Answering the Call to Teach

A Novel Approach Toward Exceptional Classroom Instruction

Charlese E. Brown

ROWMAN & LITTLEFIELD EDUCATION

A division of
ROWMAN & LITTLEFIELD PUBLISHERS, INC.
Lanham • New York • Toronto • Plymouth, UK

Published by Rowman & Littlefield Education
A division of Rowman & Littlefield Publishers, Inc.
A wholly owned subsidiary of The Rowman & Littlefield Publishing Group, Inc.
4501 Forbes Boulevard, Suite 200, Lanham, Maryland 20706
www.rowman.com

10 Thornbury Road, Plymouth PL6 7PP, United Kingdom

Copyright © 2012 by Charlese Brown

All rights reserved. No part of this book may be reproduced in any form or by any electronic or mechanical means, including information storage and retrieval systems, without written permission from the publisher, except by a reviewer who may quote passages in a review.

British Library Cataloguing in Publication Information Available

Library of Congress Cataloging-in-Publication Data
Brown, Charlese E., 1959–
  Answering the call to teach : a novel approach toward exceptional classroom instruction / Charlese Brown.
    p. cm.
  ISBN 978-1-61048-744-3 (cloth : alk. paper) — ISBN 978-1-61048-745-0 (pbk. : alk. paper) — ISBN 978-1-61048-746-7 (ebook : alk. paper)
  1. Teaching—Vocational guidance—United States. I. Title.
  LB1775.2.B75 2012
  371.1—dc23   2012006748

∞™ The paper used in this publication meets the minimum requirements of American National Standard for Information Sciences—Permanence of Paper for Printed Library Materials, ANSI/NISO Z39.48-1992.

Printed in the United States of America

*This book is dedicated to God who makes all things possible;
to my husband and best friend,
my children, my grandchildren,
my family and friends, my parents,
and the committed teachers who influenced me;
and to the thousands of students
who have taught me well throughout the years.*

I am still learning!

> How happy I am to realize that I am little and weak, how happy I am to see myself so imperfect.
>
> —Saint Theresa

Contents

Acknowledgments	vii
Introduction	1
Vocation	7

1	Changing Our National Educational Attitude toward a More Vocational Point of View	9
2	Steering Teaching toward a More Equitable Environment	15
3	Teaching with the Gift to Teach	21
4	Pursuing a Vocation	25
5	Marketing the Vocation of Teaching	31
6	Bridging the Gap in Education	39
7	Achieving Equality	45
8	Testing Teachers	51
9	Becoming Your Call	53
10	Recruiting and Retaining the Best Teachers	57
11	Making the Choice—and Sticking to It	61

Conclusion	65
Answered the Call—Made a Difference	69
Appendix	73
Notes	79
About the Author	83

Acknowledgments

Thank God for the fortitude to stick with this project.

Thanks to my family for putting up with my seclusion while dedicating my efforts to producing a book that will help lots of people.

Thanks to my parents—my first teachers.

Thanks to the many family and friends I have in the teaching profession who taught me a great deal over the years.

Thank you to Educational Design Services for recognizing the niche for and timeliness of this project.

Thank you to Rowman & Littlefield Education for a chance at having my voice heard.

May God bless you.

Introduction

Teaching is a vocation, not a profession. It should be treated as such. The challenge we face in launching our educational system into the future centers around identifying individuals who have the gift to teach.

What is a "calling?" A calling is defined as a loud cry or shout made by an animal or a person. A "calling" is also a strong urge toward a particular way of life or career—a vocation.

Have you ever heard someone say, "She looks like a doctor?" Or, "She has the hands of a great pianist?" In this life, there is a mission for each one of us. We just need to discover what it is. But, how do we discover our calling? And, why is this crucial to the world of teaching?

To discover our calling, it is necessary to experience the "ah-ha moment." When we see it, hear it, or feel it, we seem to already know it. In a classroom setting in particular, a called teacher inspires those who have the gift to teach.

A gifted teacher provides many moments of recognition for others like herself. This experience solidifies a decision and prompts it forward toward realization.

Ironically, there are thousands of students right now inside classrooms who possess the gift to teach. They feel it. They know that they have a tendency, a "pulling" if you will, toward teaching. These children with the gift to teach are in sufficient numbers—sufficient enough to fill our classrooms with great teachers. Yet, most of them choose not to teach.

What is it that makes them go against their calling? Can we do anything to help these "chosen" ones make the big leap into the classroom? A tougher question might be: how can we pave roads for people to follow their vocations?

Let's examine one obvious roadblock. In today's schools, there are too many teachers who do not belong in the classroom. These teachers are in classrooms for a variety of reasons. The most important reason, answering a call, may not be a part of the list. There are too many teachers who have chosen the teaching career assuming (or hoping) that it is their vocation. They see the job of teaching as offering a lot of perks.

Teaching accommodates family life. Along with a fairly short workday (exclusive of "extra" duties), there are two major holiday breaks with summer months fairly free.

These are the people that our children interact with on a daily basis. These are the models that have the super task of imparting new knowledge and new experiences to our children. These experiences are shaping how they think. So, what happens to the children who do not interact with the right models for the job?

More importantly, our training institutions are not vetting teacher candidates effectively. Actually, there is no vetting process at all. Anyone can choose to major in education and pursue a degree for certification. After receiving such a degree, the field is ripe for additional training and professional development.

In today's world of education, millions of dollars are being spent on professional development. These sessions will continue to fall short for our education system until we realize the importance of acquiring the people who have the gift to teach instead of those who can easily be trained to teach.

The vetting process should be analogous to what people who express an interest in religious orders go through. Without taking bias toward any religious doctrine, it may worthwhile to adapt (or at least strongly consider) some fundamental methods used to determine suitable candidates for a particular religious vocation.

Even in hospital settings, patients look for facilities with the "best" doctors. What makes these facilities the best? Hospital administrators go out of their way to pick the brightest internists and most talented doctors to serve their patients. That's how these hospitals establish a good reputation. Who wants to go to a hospital with a bad reputation?

The vetting process is all about making good common sense.

There may be something to the religious vetting process that we could use in the secular world. Before entering a convent or the priesthood, candidates go through an intensive and extensive reflective process. The reflective process concentrates on "why are you here?"

This customary process has pointed candidates in the right direction for hundreds of years. The fantastic aspect of this process is that it shows candidates what *does not* suit them.

The process of elimination is a powerful tool in getting to the right answer. When we deduct from our lives what does not serve us well, we automatically move toward a greater understanding of ourselves. We place ourselves in position to act according to our prescribed mission.

The educational standards that we presently have in place do little to help our school administrators or teachers identify persons justly suited for teaching. These standards train people to be teachers. In a subtle way, these standards may be adding to the problem.

Additionally, our standards are geared toward people who show satisfactory achievement in memorizing facts, analyzing cases (scenarios), applying general pedagogical knowledge, passing a state (or national) certification test, and satisfactorily making it through some real-life classroom experiences.

But great teaching is much more than that.

The person aptly suited to teach finds these requirements mundane and trivial to the ultimate task at hand. Would anyone interrupt Michelangelo while painting the Sistine Chapel to take an art certification test?

A football coach does not need to tell a football player with a sincere passion for the game to play his heart out. It's that "passion" (that "thing") that we need in our classrooms. Sure, the players learn and improve mechanics over time. They develop a wisdom tied to their gift. But, it's the passion that makes them great. We all have heard the stories of famous players who tell us that they knew they were meant to play ball. They say, "I wanted to do this all of my life."

Furthermore, it is imperative that we retain great teachers in the classroom for the sake of continuity. When a child enters the public school system (around age five), it is necessary that the child receive instruction from great teachers each and every year until graduation.

At present, the new teacher attrition rate is about five years. Before that fifth year (for those who make it that far), teachers confess that they give up long before walking away from the job.

It is that "giving up" period that hurts our children the most. If a person is hanging on by a thread, how can they help anyone else?

There are no experimental designs that we can adapt to identify gifted people. But, we do know that some people understand the nature of reaching children and are more successful at reaching children than others. They hold the keys to turning the tide on our failing education system.

So, how do we identify these young "gifted" people in our classrooms?

To complicate an already complicated situation, we don't. They know who they are. It's our job to put in place strategies that would make the path an easy one to access, one that would make them come toward the call.

It would probably be safe to say that if a person feels comfortable with choosing teaching, they will stay. People who answer the call to religious vocations tell us that both family and community support actually assisted them in making their decisions. Once they made that "leap of faith," they emphatically state that they found a sort of "peace" with their decision. It felt right.

A study of gifted teachers notes that "this record encouraged a belief in some people that good teaching must be purely instinctive, a kind of magic performed by born superstars."[1] It is important that we get people in front of our children who are truly gifted to teach—for a number of reasons.

1. These people are comfortable with who they are. They will act as ethical models for our children.
2. These people have an inner peace about what they do. They understand how children think. The children they teach tend to be more creative. They increase the likelihood of inquiry-based learning.
3. These people are not very likely to leave the classroom. They are committed to their calling and their passion keeps them engaged.

The dynamics of having gifted teachers in every classroom would have an immediate impact to the overall education challenge. If anyone wants to know how to raise test scores, seek out gifted teachers.

Attrition rates would decrease. Teacher absenteeism would be practically zero. There are so many advantages to having teachers who find teaching a true fulfillment.

According to Eric Hanushek, "If you 'deselect' 5% of the least effective teachers, student performance would increase about 0.35 standard deviations."[2]

The most important quality that gifted teachers bring to the classroom is patience. Without patience, anyone teaching in the classroom can hang it up. Teaching at least 20 different personalities at one time is no easy feat. It's a hard job, especially on those days when the 20 different personalities are working against the establishment. The scientific data shows us that teachers who spend more time disciplining students spend less time transferring knowledge. That time is a waste.

Having patience also comes into play when dealing with parents. Parents are an integral part of educating a child. Parents send their children to school to learn something new. This expectation can sometimes lead to high-anxiety moments.

It is no secret that when you love what you do, you will do it well.

People who answer the call to teach understand what a vocation is. It is a call to serve. Our training units should begin treating it as such. Teacher candidates should know that teaching should be a lifelong commitment. It should not be entered into lightly.

The elements that will change our education structure are:

1. Getting talented teachers in the classroom
2. Correctly vetting a teacher candidate
3. Emphasizing effective teaching through ethics
4. Eliminating unequal and unfair education practices

It is not enough to merely discuss eradicating unequal practices just in legal terms. Legal issues get caught up in court and wind up filling the halls of law libraries. However, this is not to discount the need for law. The laws that govern a fair and equal education for all children are necessary and staple components of our society.

Think of how much less time we would spend on frivolous legal matters if we had more competent people in the classroom.

So, that's where we will begin.

Vocation

- (n.) A call; a summons; a citation; especially, a designation or appointment to a particular state, business, or profession.
- (n.) Destined or appropriate employment; calling; occupation; trade; business; profession.
- (n.) The bestowment of God's distinguishing grace upon a person or nation, by which that person or nation is put in the way of salvation; as, the vocation of the Jews under the old dispensation, and of the Gentiles under the gospel.
- (n.) A call to special religious work, as to the ministry.
- (n.) A calling by the will of God.

(Read more at www.brainyquote.com/words/vo/vocation237895.html#ixzz1nfIlzK4I)

Early 15c., "spiritual calling," from L. vocationem (nom. vocatio), lit. "a calling," from *vocatus* "called," pp. of *vocare* "to call" (see voice). Sense of "one's occupation or profession" is first attested 1550s.
(Source: Online Etymology Dictionary, www.etymonline.com.)

• 1 •

Changing Our National Educational Attitude toward a More Vocational Point of View

> Cultivating awe is part of unlocking the truest sense of life's purpose.
>
> —Jonathan Haidt

Is teaching for everyone? The answer is definitely "no." If we care about what our children learn, who teaches them, and how well they learn, then it is critical that we have a frank discussion about the teaching profession and the entire education system as it exists today.

Talented teachers can make the difference. People who answer their true calls in life become that role. A talented surgeon has special hands. Some would call those hands "gifted." When musicians are self-taught, we celebrate that. We pay huge sums of money for good seats. How often do we tell a person, "You are meant to be a teacher"? Or, "You have a knack for teaching children"?

Some gifts "rub off" merely by being "close" to a person with a gift. This association alone makes an impact. Every now and again we hear from famous singers who tell us their stories. In a number of cases, they tell us that they are products of parents who play music or sing as well. Maybe the genetic factor is in play here. Who knows?

One thing that's true—being around someone who is gifted tends to give another person a "tendency" or advantage toward that gift. The least that happens is that the person gets some exposure to what being gifted "feels" like. Of course, this may be somewhat empirical knowledge. But, the results are very real.

There are some people who are truly born to teach. No matter how many classroom observations are made of exceptional teachers, those who are not born to teach will never make great teachers. It's that simple. No amount of training can resolve this issue for people without the gift.

There is a lot of money being spent on programs that disseminate information to classroom teachers. School districts discover that fact (painfully so) after their budget needs balancing—only to recognize that there is little room to include other necessary programs.

Making a difference in the schools today means that we locate, identify, and encourage gifted people to enter into the classroom. Religious groups have a variety of methods of identifying people who have the "call."

Let's examine the key points to vetting a candidate for the religious life:[1]

1. Extensive interviews
2. Background checks
3. Medical testing
4. Psychological testing
5. Live-in "community"
6. Observe a certain level of maturity
7. Expectation of living up to the rigor of the vocation

When we look at these criteria, we can clearly see how they can be contrasted with what we have in place for training teachers.

1. Extensive interviews: candidates do not interview to enter as an education major.
2. Background checks: candidates do not have background checks done when scheduling education classes.
3. Medical testing: routine medical testing may be done. Vaccinations are a requirement under the law.
4. Psychological testing: may be done by some schools to determine potentially suicidal students.
5. Live-in community: candidates get in-class experience through student teaching. This experience only allows them to observe or participate in a limited fashion.
6. Observe a certain level of maturity: this is "assumed" for all candidates wishing to be teachers.
7. Expectation of living up to the rigor of the vocation: candidates are required to pass a state certification test.

As you can tell, there is a lot of work to do to pull up our requirements of getting the "right" teacher in the classroom.

For instance, medical schools have methods of interviewing possible candidates that gives the interviewing board a glimpse into knowing if they have a potentially "gifted" doctor in their midst. These higher levels of academia deliberately seek out exceptional candidates.

So, why don't we spend that kind of energy toward selecting teachers? Teachers are responsible for a large chunk of our children's education from ages five through eighteen.

According to the Organization for Economic Cooperation and Development data from 2008, teachers spend over 1000 contact hours per school year with our children. This number reflects classroom instruction and not time spent at home or involved in after-school programs.[2]

Teaching is one of the most important jobs that we have in this country. If done right, good teaching will have a far-reaching impact on our society and our ability to compete on a global level.[3]

At present, we have no component in place to determine whether a teacher candidate was born to teach. The current model centers on these criteria: Have you passed the state test? Do you have a college degree? Do you have teaching experience? How long have you been a teacher? Instead, we should be asking:

1. What did your parents do?
2. When you were in third grade, what did you want to be?
3. Did you ever pretend being a teacher as a child?
4. Where did you go to elementary school? Which teacher influenced you to teach?
5. How many people in your family are teachers?
6. Can you imagine doing anything else in life besides teaching?
7. What do you think is your gift?

Here's the thing—there are a lot of people who are born to teach. It is actually fascinating to recognize this talent in the classroom among children who have the gift to teach. Some students are bold with this gift. Sometimes, they are misunderstood and labeled as troublemakers.

Too often, they are discounted. In a very subtle way, they are discouraged from answering the call to teach by people who are not equipped with the insight to recognize this gift.

What are some reasons that prevent gifted students from answering the call to teach?

Money is probably the number one reason. A teacher's salary is one of the main obstacles standing in the way of gifted people making a difference in the classroom.

High school teacher	$43,427
Elementary school teacher	$40,043
Middle school teacher	$41,888
Special education teacher, preschool, kindergarten, or elementary school	$40,905
Special education teacher, secondary school	$43,796
Secondary school teacher	$41,687
Special education teacher, middle school	$41,692[4]

Compare this to the salary of a physician:

Family physician/doctor	$164,311
General surgeon	$225,000
Pediatrician, general	$95,000[5]

When young people are deciding what they want to do, they understand that having enough money in which to live is a huge factor. The fact that we live in a largely materialistic world causes money to be a central issue in the decision-making process. Peer pressure is another factor. When young people share with each other what they plan to do later in life, careers with the more impressive headlines are mentioned first.

Family and community support is another factor. Family has a profound influence on career decisions. According to Taylor, Harris, and Taylor, "People who have answered the call to vocations express to us that it was the support of their families that helped them to take that 'next' step."[6]

Every one of us can recall that special teacher who changed or shaped our lives—that person who stood head and shoulders above the others. When you think of that person, you can feel where you were, you can see that person as if the moment is now, and you can describe the difference that person made in your life.

Gifted teachers identify others with the gift. This is one way in which we can continue the cycle. Our "great" teachers can help us—not by observing them in order to duplicate their methods to develop new teaching standards, but by allowing them to create environments that support children—especially those who feel a calling to teach.

Every day, inside the classroom, children have exposure to teaching as a vocation. Every time a teacher speaks, a child is influence in one direction or the other. Sometimes, it may just take a simple word of notice to a student that sparks an interest in teaching or validates what the child already feels is her calling.

Parents, who understand the difference having a great teacher makes, seek schools where gifted teachers are plentiful. So, what we have as a result is a lopsided system in which the students who are left behind get the "satisfactory" teachers (usually products of rigorous training) and the "best students" who are in schools get the best teachers.

As a result, we all lose. We lose out in attracting gifted students who one day would make great teachers, and we lose at producing the best students possible—those ready for global competition.

Additionally, the best schools are usually too expensive for the majority of the public to afford. We can change that. We should change that. We do not have to control the cost of what these schools charge, but we need to change the accessibility of the great teachers to the entire population of students.

The future of our nation's capacity to compete on a global level depends on it. This would accomplish two things: (1) inspiring gifted children to answer their calling and (2) creating an environment where original thinking takes place.

• *2* •

Steering Teaching toward a More Equitable Environment

> Teaching middle school is not for the faint of heart. But if you're called to do it, you know there's nothing else quite like it.
>
> —Edutopia.org

*D*espite the "highly qualified" status that our states impose on teachers, the students are still failing. The resources that education agents offer are not helping. Some positive "bumps" in statistics are observed, but the long-range goals are in the fog. No one can predict the success of current methods.

There is only blind hope. The education system continues being peeled away like an onion. Piece by piece, politicians and state legislatures are stripping away the "spirit" of education. The spirit of education is slowly leaving our country only because the number of great teachers is diminishing.

The bureaucratic nature of acquiring accurate factual textbooks, the legal restrictions of districts, and local control over teachers and administrators all work together to take the "flavor" out of the classroom. So, how do we recapture the spirit of innovation?

First, let's take a look at the changes in mathematics. Some experts argue that children should not be asked to memorize multiplication tables.[1] The claim is that if children are shown how multiplication was "invented," then it will free up mental space in order to actually utilize the process of multiplication. Anyone would admit the task of memorizing multiplication tables is daunting. Some children never get the hang of it.

For instance, it is a "soft" requirement that science teachers plan for at least two laboratory activities per week. The idea is to get the tactile part of learning in front of the students. The goal is to use activities that would groom critical thinking skills. Thus, hands-on activities now rule.[2]

Children like to know "why?" If a teacher can teach the subject while reaching the "why" factor, then the students have an awesome experience in the classroom. That teacher "gets" how to make connections.

This is the work of a great teacher. With that said, students need to understand the background of the concepts before being introduced to practice problems. Consider Egyptian math for a moment.

A child can be introduced to the "wow" of math simply by understanding where the numbers come from and what can be done with them. Egyptian math dates back to 3000 BC. It is based on counting by tens (like the metric system). Egyptian math covered all bases: addition, fractions, algebra, and geometry. The Egyptians devised fractions and the binary system, and used geometry to settle challenges like building pyramids.[3] Can you imagine that word problem?

Most of the subjects students take in school give some background before jumping into the lesson: science—early experiments; social studies—Pangaea, migration, occupations, wars, colonization, and culture; economics—history of early commerce, governing, and trading; English—etymology of words, early writings.

However when it comes to numbers, we just jump right into the task, omitting the history of numbers.

If we would take the time to teach the base ten operations at an early age, we could save our children a lot of headaches. Filling in this gap will enable children to have something on which to fall back on when the calculator or cash register gives out. The more difficult math classes would make more sense.

A stronger understanding of math would automatically result in a stronger grasp of science and lead to a desire to want to learn more. Too many students complain that math is "too hard." That's because hardly anyone takes the time to show them how beautiful math can be. We cannot exist in this world without numbers.

Have you heard that spelling no longer counts? Yes, in some instances, students are not penalized for misspelled words. In the world of "getting it done" for testing purposes, some schools have opted out of the "trivial" matters like spelling.[4]

Only a few years back, teachers were required to teach phonics. We had many tools and kits to help children learn how to pronounce words and how to sound them out. Well, that's gone—for the most part. Anyone who knows anything about processing skills knows that language takes a lot of processing cells. What are we doing by shutting down these processing skills?

A child's reading level is directly affected by the inability of that child to sound out words. Doesn't that make sense? Who wants to read if they cannot? There is a definite need for teaching phonics in our schools. This is one component that should be a staple part to educating any child.

Running concurrently with omitting phonics is eliminating teaching handwriting skills. Hand-to-eye coordination is vital to laying the foundation of future skills. Part of a teacher's frustration comes from the variety of skill levels that children entering school have. In pre-Kindergarten, only a handful of children come to school "ready."

Researchers have blamed the parents, lack of resources, and environment for children falling behind. The one constant in this mix is the teacher. A child should be able to enter "behind and be given individualized instruction in order to catch up."

Instead, teachers take a lot out on the child who comes ill prepared. Early on, the child drops out long before he actually drops out. Somewhere between third and fourth grade, a child knows and feels if he is going to do well in school. This is the "window" of time in which children make a lot of decisions. Some of these include: What am I going to be in life? How do I see myself? A child knows as early as first grade what his true calling is.

It's in the primary grades where the solution to the dropout rates in America should begin. It is important to instill the value of an education into a child right away, before he allows failing to be his norm.

Lastly, where has the equal sign gone? In someone's haste to solve the nation's problem in mathematics, the equal sign went away. Notice—the word haste was mentioned. Patchwork will not solve the problem.

Our nation's schools are bleeding. It will take radical surgery to save them. To all of the "new" math people, there is nothing wrong with leaving the equal sign alone. This sign is a staple member of our society.

We need equality teaching in every classroom. Children see through this. Sometimes, it's the simple things that we miss that can wind up making so much of a difference in the classroom.

When we finally come to terms with refusing to dilute the material that our children have to learn, we will be halfway to the goal line. The other half is recognizing that we have to insist on excellence instead of mediocrity. Too often, teachers teach to "certain" children over others.

Of course, it is a joy teaching those children who want to learn. The difficulty comes in getting Johnny to care. This apathy could be coming from anywhere—home life, pressures on the playground, general health, lack of self-esteem—the list can go on.

Teachers should be able to rise above those problems.

The expectation that we have of new teachers is sometimes referred to as the "savior" mentality. But, each and every child puts teachers into that role.

This should be a point of concern when choosing candidates with a strong passion to teach. At our training institutions, candidates need a clear understanding of their role in the classroom.

Education majors study how people learn and how to best teach them. Classes cover such topics as educational psychology, school health and safety issues, and the planning of classroom activities. Most colleges, universities, and alternative certification programs require the following:[5]

- 12 hours of English, science, and math
- Teaching reading
- Special education
- History/social studies
- Clinical hours
- Teacher internship/seminar
- Effective teaching
- Curriculum and methods

When we examine why teachers are leaving the field, we have to include the preparation into the analysis. There is no way anyone could be expected to handle children with this type of "guidance." If we dare to allow our logical senses to take over for a brief moment, then we may be able to envision a new sort of teacher preparation program.

Let's consider the following:

- Three years (15 credits) of field internship (includes mentorship and tutorial requirement)
- Two years (12 credits) of school law
- Two years (12 credits) of philosophy (including ethics)
- One year (6 credits) of English
- Two years (12 credits) of independent study (special education)
- Two years (12 credits) of history/social studies
- One year (6 credits) of pedagogy
- One year (6 credits) of curriculum
- Two years (12 credits) of practical psychology (including an "identity" class)
- Four years (24 credits) of portfolio presentation (under a committee of instruction and including personality test results)
- Three credits of art history
- Total credits = 120

Take note of the remedy. There is less emphasis on courses that merely consume time and more emphasis placed on actually understanding the nature of teaching as a vocation. The second set of choices allows a teacher candidate to explore the classroom, his own skill set and what is expected of a teacher in the real world.

The unique part of the proposed correction of courses is that teacher candidates would be required to submit a detailed portfolio upon graduation. A committee of instruction will review this portfolio. It should cover every year spent in the education program along with extensive reflection for each year, supported by citations.

Our preparation units can adopt a new vision. We have to if our children are to compete at a global level and if we want our teachers to be the best in the world.

• 3 •

Teaching with the Gift to Teach

Patience is the companion of wisdom. What does love look like? It has the hands to help others. It has the feet to hasten to the poor and needy. It has the eyes to see misery and want. It has the ears to hear the sighs and sorrows of men. That's what love looks like.

—St. Augustine

Exceptional instruction of a child begins before birth. At birth, no matter the color, creed, or character, each person has the same needs: shelter, food, clothing, air, and water. For the first four or five years of a child's life, she is at home or at a nursery facility. Around age five, children begin formal school training.

Are we missing children with the gift to teach because of our present school structure? Are we setting gifted children behind before they even enter school?

Most people agree that the first teachers of a child are the parents. So, what happens if the parents are not there? What happens if the parents do not know how to parent?

In a teaching environment, these are things out of our control. We can make judgments about lifestyles and how this influences children, but the bottom line is that we must work within the parameters of what is in our control.

Our primary teachers are essential to this effort. At school, a child who comes from an adverse home life should be made to feel like a precious gem.

What are the characteristics of a gifted teacher? People with the gift to teach:

- Are comfortable in their own skins
- Embrace innovation
- Stir inquiry
- Fully understand the nature of the "true" question, not necessarily the question being asked
- Can reach all students at once
- Possess above-average competency in subject area
- Have a variety of outside interests (not confined to the classroom)
- Are open to learning
- Are open to academic challenges
- Relax well
- Are comfortable with hard-to-reach students
- Have very minimal (to no) prejudices/biases
- Recognize strengths of children in a classroom
- Recognize weaknesses of children in a classroom
- Groom future teachers
- Are not afraid to admit errors/can correct themselves in public
- Are excellent communicators (written and oral)
- Can laugh about themselves with others
- Are exceptional storytellers
- Facilitate instruction
- Are not afraid to take unconventional routes to teach a child
- Are tolerant beyond measure

These qualities are not taught in college. These are qualities that draw children toward teachers. These are qualities that separate great teachers from satisfactory teachers. Some courses may supply some experience in critical areas, like speaking before an audience and communicating with peers.

What are people saying about great teachers?

> A teacher needs a sense of humor to counteract all the nonsense she has to take from students; she needs infinite patience; she needs a lot of energy; she must be a well-organized person. Of course, she needs to have a thorough knowledge of her subject matter and the willingness to upgrade that knowledge throughout her teaching career.
>
> My most favorite teachers had a number of the following qualities:
> - Thorough knowledge of the material being taught
> - Ability to explain the material clearly and in different ways
> - Willingness to always answer questions, even from a student who's a slacker and comes to class once a year

- An interest in the subject being taught that goes beyond the level at which the subject is being taught
- Ability to pose questions that are both interesting and challenging
- Ability to be consistent with their rubric/policy
- Open to suggestions from students, but having the wisdom to not bend to students' will
- Ability to keep everything in perspective and not go into a panic attack every time a student copies homework/calls out/comes late to class
- Love for the profession

The best teachers are the ones that have patience and understanding with a child's needs. Understanding that all kids are not the same and learn in a variety of different ways, a teacher that can adjust to that.

A good teacher gives respect to his/her students, which earns respect from the students and can build relationships built on that respect. Then real, relevant teaching can take place.

Compassionate, caring, understands room for improvement, creative, firm and consistent, patient, organized, connects with students.[1]

• 4 •

Pursuing a Vocation

> It is the supreme art of the teacher to awaken joy in creative expression and knowledge.
>
> —Albert Einstein

Pursuing a vocation is a wonderful feeling. Doing what you are truly meant to be doing here on this planet frees your mind and enables you to totally engage in a fulfilling mission of service. There are a lot of people who may not view teaching as a career in service, but that is what's at the core of being a great teacher.

This is a somewhat novel way of looking at teaching. For years, we have considered teaching a profession, a job. But teaching is much more than that. When you consider the entire scope of how many lives teachers touch every day, it becomes apparent that we must design methods that will give us the crème of the crop.

On an average, most teachers come into contact with 20–100 children per school year. That's a lot of lives. If the average attrition rate is five years, then that means a "bad" teacher can affect the outcome of 100–500 children during her time teaching. If we multiplied that number by the hundreds of thousands of teachers, we get millions of children with less than adequate instruction every year. The outcome of children not receiving an adequate education has ramifications both in the private lives of these people and in their potential contributions to society.

When we examine school data, it is clear that there is a great need for a new method of securing our children's future. Figure 4.1 shows children ages 16–18 who were not enrolled in school in 2010:

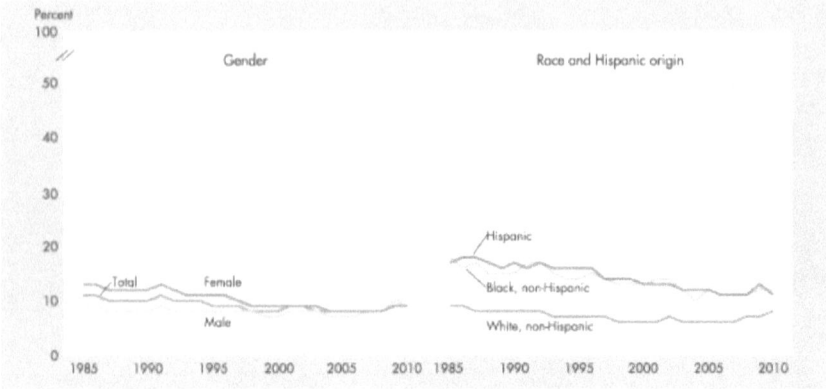

Figure 4.1. Percentage of Youth Ages 16–19 Neither Enrolled in School Nor Working, by Gender and Race, 1985–2010

The figure shows that dropouts consist of:

- 9% of all adolescents 16–19
- 11% of Hispanic children
- 12% of black (non-Hispanic) children
- 8% of white children

Where are these children? How are they getting lost from the system? How can we stop the bleeding? Nine percent translates into hundreds of thousands of children. If our standards are high and our training units are turning out capable teachers, then we should be seeing a dramatic decrease in the number of children who want to skip the entire academic phase of their lives.

In an *Atlantic* article, Amanda Ripley notes, "But we have never identified excellent teachers in any reliable, objective way. Instead, we tend to ascribe their gifts to some mystical quality that we can recognize and revere—but not replicate. The great teacher serves as a hero but never, ironically, as a lesson."[1]

A great teacher is a called teacher. Our science falls short of successfully "replicating" great teachers, not because we cannot replicate what we see, but because the people who take the charge cannot successfully deliver the responses in a duplicate manner.

For example, when a football coach shows the team a fundamental drill, he looks for those players who can execute the drill naturally. The other players repeat the skill, hoping that they will be able to master it. A percentage of people will never be able to pull off the skills.

What we have here is a career that fundamentality relies on something that cannot be easily explained. However, the people who can really do the job well cannot explain how it happens.

Maybe it's not as important to force duplication as it is identifying people with the gift to teach. In an odd sort of way, great teachers do possess something "magical," but that is not a bad thing. Exceptional instructors take fundamental knowledge and extrapolate that knowledge into a realm beyond the norm.

Our concentration on duplicating methods used by great teachers will fall short of the mark. Staff development costs money. School districts spend countless dollars hiring education consultants to host seminars for teachers who need help. These teachers return to the classroom. For a while, the newly learned techniques seem to work. After some time elapses, the students can fall back into the same pattern and the teacher begins to operate under the umbrella of frustration. All in all, the money is wasted—not to mention the time.

The American Education Research Association (AERA) describes staff development in this way:

> To be effective, professional development must provide teachers with a way to directly apply what they learn to their teaching. Research shows that professional development leads to better instruction and improved student learning when it connects to the curriculum materials that teachers use, the district and state academic standards that guide their work, and the assessment and accountability measures that evaluate their success.[2]

The AERA defines the components of professional development to include:

- Mentoring
- Required in-service days
- Professional conferences
- Technology training
- Master's degree
- Subject area team meetings
- Common planning time
- Grade-level meetings
- Induction programs
- Support for lead/master teachers
- School-based coaching
- Advanced certification

Is staff development effective? Does our system train candidates in a teacher certification program and then train them again once on the job? Could it be that this redundancy is creating confusion? Case in point: in medical school, the students learn the fundamentals of their craft. Internships provide real-life experiences. After a doctor completes residency, she may attend professional conferences, join professional communities, and read the latest in medical advances.

For too many teachers, staff development is relearning the fundamentals over and over again. The methods of teaching change so much that the data for effectiveness is difficult to assess. Local districts get to choose which areas of development are right for them.

In numerous cases, these areas may be unchanged for years. The overall dropout rate is clear evidence that what we have currently in place is not working. Additionally, staff development is doing little to improve teacher effectiveness.

Teachers know who the great teachers are.

As far as costs are concerned, the cost for staff development is approximately 3% to 5% of the total operating cost of a local district. This means that every year, hundreds of thousands of dollars is being spent on training teachers or enhancing teachers' knowledge.[3]

Staff development includes:

- Planning in-service programs
- Delivering in-service programs
- Covering costs for an additional 2–3 day "before" school opening
- Workshops for staff
- Reimbursing tuition
- Personnel evaluations and support
- Covering salary increases

The Truly Great Teachers

The percentage of teachers who say:

* In my building, it is easy to spot who the truly great teachers are: 78%
* Most teachers in my building could pretty much agree on who the great teachers are: 72%
* Hard to tell: 16%

Source: "Stand By Me: What Teachers Really Think about Unions, Merit Pay and Other Professional Matters." Public Agenda, 2003, http://publicagenda.org/files/pdf/stand_by_me.pdf.

It would probably be safe to say that due to the cost we put into duplicating methods from great teachers, the high attrition rate, and the lack of significant graduation growth, our education system is headed in the wrong direction.

Why don't we allow the great teachers to be great? The notion that someone can enter the classroom and count the number of steps, the number of smiles, the number of greetings, the number of times conversations are held is a bit cumbersome. There is no way the same methods will work for any two or more people.

The classroom dynamics are different for each case. The children are different. And, more importantly, the children will respond differently to two different people. It may come down to a person's voice inflections or her style of dress.

The children know the difference. The attributes they think are important to having a great classroom environment are outlined in this book.

• 5 •

Marketing the Vocation of Teaching

> We need to internalize this idea of excellence. Not many folks spend a lot of time trying to be excellent.
>
> —Barack Obama

(Reuters)—A majority of U.S. high school students say they get bored in class every day, and more than one out of five has considered dropping out, according to a survey released on Wednesday.

The survey of 81,000 students in 26 states found two-thirds of high school students complain of boredom, usually because the subject matter was irrelevant or their teachers didn't seem to care about them.... Half of the students surveyed said they had skipped school without a valid excuse at least once, and 22 percent said they had considered dropping out. More than half said they spent an hour or less per week reading and studying.

Yet, three of four students surveyed said they expected to earn a high school diploma and go on to college.[1]

Approximately 30% of students indicate they are bored due to lack of interaction with teachers and 75% report material being taught is not interesting.[2]

The ordinary classroom has desks modeled after the first desks used in the United States public schools since the late 1800s. Most classrooms have no windows. Not enough rooms have sufficient activity centers or extra space. Basically, teachers are as creative as they can be under the circumstances.

How would we begin to tackle a marketing strategy to promote the notion that teachers have to be people who have the gift to teach and who should answer the call to teach? We know that honesty, sincerity, and reliability sell products. If what is advertised does what it claims to do, then people will buy into it and the marketing campaign is a success.

This mission starts off with advertising. It may sound odd. But planting the seed is important. Having strong role models is definitely a plus. Children must "see" this in order to understand what teaching is supposed to be in the classroom. Children must see that they have a portal to interact with teachers as well as other children in the classroom. They must see a classroom as a least restrictive environment. They must see classrooms as a place where ideas are born, questions are raised, and thoughts are discussed without fear.

Making a claim about pursuing a vocation to teach should flow easily since there are a lot of children who are interested in becoming teachers. Also, teachers are already in a position to recognize students with this gift. If a teacher is truly in touch with her students, it is easy to select those students who would make excellent classroom instructors.

Here are a few guidelines for identifying children with the gift to teach.

- Does the child volunteer to help others with their work in class?
- Does the child reorganize the teacher's work or make suggestions concerning logistics in the classroom?
- Does the child oversee the good of the class as a whole?
- Does the child like to hang around with teachers?
- Does the child like to give speeches?
- Does the child have a commanding voice when speaking?
- Does the child like to have his parents come to school?
- Does the child join community-type projects at the school?

These questions are a foundational tool to use to sift out children who may one day become great teachers.

Next, colleges have to be open up to changing the traditional methods of training in order to accept talented students and take them further than what is expected on a state and federal level. For instance, teacher candidates will have to understand that they may discover the teaching profession is not their calling. Teacher candidates will also need to investigate their own character to determine if they are indeed good candidates for the vocation of teaching.

The marketing campaign must include getting children to buy into education along the way. The best way to do this is to have talented teachers as role models that the children come in contact with on a daily basis. That's the real sell!

This sell does not include paying children to go to school. Value should be the message. Do it because it is the right thing to do. We must instill a moral compass along the way.

Children can work at classroom activities and enjoy the work. The symbiotic relationship between the teacher and the student sets the stage for solving problems, working in teams, and generating original ideas.

A simple earth science lesson on groundwater can turn from a notetaking experience to actually building a model with sand and clay and feeding water underground. The students can be asked to solve the problem of polluting our groundwater system by using their models and presenting their thoughts before the class.

Any teacher using worksheets today is not using the correct marketing strategy. These children will not be able to extrapolate the information they learn in the classroom to the outside world. Once they step outside of the door, the information has no relevance and no value.

Teachers want to know that the students are talking about their classroom experiences among each other. If the students are not sharing, then a key part of the marketing process has been lost.

Marketing strategies for the classroom include:

- Honesty
- Fairness
- Depth
- Motivation/inspiration
- Sharing
- Cooperation
- A support system

Let's examine these separately.

Honesty plays a huge part in a child's life, no matter the age. If a teacher says something to a child, it's basically the gospel truth. Take what we purchase at the grocery stores, for example. Our purchases reflect not only our needs, but also what we've been persuaded to buy. If a certain detergent does not really clean like the advertisement proclaims, then that detergent will stay on the shelf the next time around.

Children look for the honest approach first. They can sense if a teacher is an honest person in her personal life. It's one of the things that children do. They instinctively know. Teachers must deliver content honestly. If a teacher knows that the class does not like word problems, it's probably better to open the class with that acknowledgement instead of saying, "You should like word problems. They're fun."

The dynamics of the class just shifted from the student-centered focus to the teacher talking to herself. The students hear that statement as: "She's not listening. Does she really care what I think? It's a good time to go to sleep."

All concepts will not automatically make students gravitate toward them. We have to give pause to *a priori* statements like "word problems are hard." They are getting this information from somewhere. Otherwise, how could they be so judgmental about a word problem they have never seen?

What manufacturers do to sell new products before mass producing the product is to test-market it. A fast food chain may advertise a particular sandwich and track how well it is received by the public. If enough people purchase the sandwich in that area, then the store adopts that sandwich. It seems like a pretty simple process.

This method involves "throwing" the concepts out there. Allow students the room to judge, but give them parameters. Here's an example: if a student does not like word problems, instruct her to write an essay explaining why, and that the essay must answer:

- Where did I first encountered a word problem?
- When have I done word problems before?
- What else would I substitute for a word problem if I were in charge?
- Have I ever encountered a word problem in my daily life?

If this approach is too unrealistic for some children, then a teacher can easily put some of these questions before a student in a one-on-one conference, and specifically a parent conference. The focal point is to show the student that they encounter and solve word problems in their daily everyday lives.

Fairness is a major issue inside the classroom. Children notice the slightest difference. If the activity calls for 10 wooden craft sticks and the teacher makes a mistake and gives one group slightly more sticks, the children notice. If something as small as this is noticed, then teachers must go through extensive lengths to assure children that fairness is the number-one policy and the law of the land. Teachers must pay attention to all children when looking out into the audience, address everybody the same, and take notice of what children do.

When it comes to consequences, fairness is a big concern for children. The students look for consistency. Teachers must govern the entire class under the same rules and avoid playing favorites. This does not mean that the "all for one" philosophy is in effect. Teachers make serious mistakes when they punish the entire class for the wrongs of one or two students. Children interpret this as gross negligence. The disruptive students have won in this case. Teachers should use these moments to teach children that fairness counts and those who are responsible for a wrong should expect consequences.

Children learn early that life is not fair. When they come to school at about age five, they should be in environments that foster caring. Too often, they fall victim to adults who experienced unfairness as a child and who may unconsciously project those "fears" to the class.

Earlier it was mentioned that teachers should undergo a psychological reflection before entering the classroom. This does not imply that people who want to be teachers have psychological problems, but that may be the case in some instances. It would certainly be better for everyone concerned if we knew before these people enter a classroom.

Depth of knowledge for teachers is a big concern for the community, parents, and other stakeholders. A teacher must go beyond her field of expertise to gain more knowledge in fields that do not really interest her. A great teacher reads from a variety of sources. Any math teacher should be able to help with English homework. A student may not expect a teacher to know everything, but enough to say, "I don't know. But I know where to go to find the answer." A student respects that and will trust that teacher.

Depth and breath of knowledge also opens up an inquiry-based learning environment. If a teacher reads a lot, then she will be likely to press her students to do the same. These teachers present material that connects real-world experiences to class-based instruction. Conversations begin and critical thinking occurs.

In this environment, children feel free to express their ideas and true "knowledge trading" takes place. These classrooms have:

- Fewer behavior problems
- More participation
- Increased interest
- More autonomy
- Teachers as facilitators

Motivation and inspiration go hand in hand. Teachers know that every child will not respond. And, that is fine. Flowers bloom at different rates. It may not be a bad thing for a child to not gravitate toward a teacher who is a strong motivator. Here's the deal—the experiences will make a difference in the child's future.

Motivation does not mean entertainment. Too often teachers feel as if they have to entertain children to gain their attention. This is not true. Before a child goes to school, she already has in her mind that the routine is mundane. So, anything outside of the norm is a plus.

Motivational techniques are simple. Here's a list of 20 motivational techniques to use in the classroom:

1. Encourage internal motivation
2. Plan assignments that are neither too easy or too difficult
3. Explain purpose behind assignment
4. Create realistic goals
5. Lead by example
6. Tell stories
7. Incorporate student experiences
8. Respond to students' interests
9. Show interest in students as individuals
10. Promote open communication and discussion
11. Allow students to help
12. Create special traditions
13. Give sincere praise
14. Build confidence
15. Encourage curiosity
16. Guide students
17. Allow students to explore
18. Promote teamwork
19. Tailor rewards to individuals
20. Make sure all students feel included[3]

Sharing is a quality that is usually taught at the kindergarten level and in the primary grades. Teachers may even find that middle and high school students do like sharing supplies in the classroom. The value system in place must reflect full cooperation in order for the teacher to be successful. In general, students will follow examples of good sharing practices. Sharing skills add to the value of classroom learning.

Children have to be taught the best way to cooperate with other. At times, competition may get in the way. Teachers must cooperate with each other as well. Cooperative group learning has been a key player for at least the past 20 years in getting students in touch with concepts in a real-world fashion. Cooperative group learning puts the student in charge.

A strong support system is crucial to teaching, especially for children who come from unsupportive home environments. Today's buzzword, "poverty," has schools responding to children in a negative way.

There is nothing about being poor that can be tied to intelligence. The problem is the education issue is so complex that some people see in the data what they want to see. When pioneers at some schools make phenomenal gains in test scores and manage to turn the school around, it is considered an "exception" to the rule.

People flock around that teacher or that administrator to observe what makes her so successful. The financial status of a family should have no bearing on a child's ability to learn—if the proper components are in place at the school.

Children know about judgment. They may not openly express how they feel, but they know. Teachers, school administrators, and school districts must take care not to single children out to the point where they feel uncomfortable. For example, there may be a particular program at the school and the teacher needs a quick overview of which students are eligible. To be eligible, the student has to receive free or reduced lunch. To avoid looking up the information, the teachers asks the class, "Who receives free and reduced lunch?" Generally, this is a harmless question. But there may be some students who refuse to show their hand despite the rewards of the new program. Having a thoughtful support system in place is invaluable.

Some elements of cooperative learning are:

- Promoting student learning and academic achievement
- Increasing student retention
- Enhancing student satisfaction with their learning experience
- Helping students develop skills in oral communication
- Developing students' social skills
- Promoting student self-esteem
- Helping to promote positive race relations[4]

Temporary agencies work on the "best fit" model. If a position at an office building is open, the agency looks for the best fit. We tend to do this with the majority of our careers. Why should teaching be any different?

Parents have to know that talking to their children about becoming a teacher is all right. We should not allow this type of encouragement to fall too far off the radar screen—like farming has. Families do not tend to encourage their children to be farmers when they grow up. Somehow, that is a "bad" choice. Yet, we need to eat every day.

Becoming a teacher has to be in the conversation. Becoming a teacher has to be a part of electives in high school. Now, this is not to be confused with the way families in some countries take children from almost infancy and decide what the child will be for the rest of his life. What is being suggested here is that we help children to discover their true roles in this life. If that role is to become a teacher, then it is incumbent upon us to make certain that the child has every resource necessary to be the best teacher.

An integral part of the marketing strategy should include cooperation. Children should be taught how to cooperate with each other. Teaching is one of those jobs that force you to work with other people. So, being a "people" person is essential to the job.

No one would argue that a key element to successful marketing is knowing the target audience. This includes surveying the clients (students), networking with peers (other great teachers), and becoming a global player (being top of your academic game).

It also includes knowing the audience well enough to alter plans, consider revising strategies, and allowing the client (student) to share responsibility in the decision-making processes.

Great teachers are going to make the difference in our classrooms. These people have what it takes, what every expert agrees, to be the solution to what ails our education platform.

• 6 •

Bridging the Gap in Education

> Give a man a fish and you feed him for a day. Teach a man to fish and you feed him for a lifetime.
>
> —Chinese proverb

Do you know your "hidden bias?" Project Implicit[1] (created by psychologists from Harvard University, University of Virginia, and University of Washington) should be a staple requirement of every school district to assess whether an applicant can teach in a diverse learning environment. The project's Implicit Association Tests have come under fire for the validity and reproducibility of results. However, the tests can give an accurate picture of what may lie beneath the surface.

Disparities exist in classroom instruction, in part, because of the hidden biases of teachers. Studies show that some teachers teach more to boys than girls, pay more attention to smart children over difficult children, and impart hidden biases to children. These biases belong at the foundation of the disparities that children experience during classroom instruction.

Children sense hidden biases. They see that some teachers teach:

- More to boys than girls
- More to persons of European decent over other races
- More to smarter students over disruptive students

These prejudices go undetected each and every day, mainly because we don't know enough about deciphering the signals, or we turn our heads away when given enough knowledge to put some actions in place that would ensure our children are being taught by the best teachers. Awareness of bias offers more support to the notion that teacher candidates need to go through more intense self-evaluating courses before embarking into the world of teaching.

Training units tackle the professional knowledge and skills level components of teaching standards very effectively. However, children see teachers in a different light. There is no faster way to limit a child's potential than putting a teacher with numerous hidden biases in the classroom. Hands down, this supports the need for talented teachers answering the call to teach. People who are called to teach do not expend energy on judging children based on color, creed, lifestyle, or gender. People who are called to teach are solely interested in imparting knowledge, because they are passionate about that. They find that joy comes from being an integral part of what other people learn. And people involved in following a vocation consider inner joy high on the list of "things to do."

The goal is to encourage the thirst for knowledge—not discourage it. What is not shown in the data is the influence that students who drop out of school have on students who wish to continue going to school.

A summary of the standards as set forth by the National Council of Accreditation for Teacher Education (NCATE) is:

- Knowledge and skills
- Professional dispositions
- Field experience
- Diversity[2]

There is an unspoken undercurrent that pulls children downward. Professional disposition as taught by NCATE is drowned out by the noise of silence. As strong as this voice is in influencing outcomes, the voice of great teachers can prove to be more powerful in eradicating the negative hold on our children.

Our nation has to recognize that it is what we are NOT saying that's hurting our progress toward global competition. The training units are not focusing on teaching as a vocation, but rather on methods taught to individuals who may not possess the gift to teach.

The standards are based on past data and do not include the fact that in another generation, each person on the planet will own at least one electronic device. The practical field experience that teacher candidates receive does not adequately prepare them for the real world of the classroom—or the future world of education. Hence, the high attrition rate becomes a natural consequence.

Traditionally, when a teacher is found to be less than competent, one of the first strategies that a school would take to correct this deficit is to set up a time when the teacher can attend staff development. This training comes with a monetary cost. Usually, the school absorbs the cost.

Months later, the teacher still has the problem. The administrators are left baffled and the students are worse off than before. Time and money are both wasted. Of course, student achievement is sacrificed trying to make a person what she is not meant to be.

What's important to note here is that it is not a crime to discover that a person is not suited for teaching. This discovery is good for our children, especially if the person is currently employed as a teacher. Every school year, school districts are desperate to fill vacancies with anyone who has the minimal qualifications.

The children cannot be happy if the teacher is not happy.

The evidence of our school problem being an intrinsic one is all too telling in the dropout rate (see table 6.1). Obviously, students are not happy. Otherwise, they would come to school.

Students claim that school is too boring. So, teachers resort to the notion that they have to entertain children in order to attract their attention. This is a drastic mistake. This approach offends children and aggravates them. Also, the response is not engaging. Ironically, the students retreat from complying. So, the task of getting students back on track becomes an insurmountable challenge.

A truly engaged teacher, one who is meant to teach, does not experience this problem. Her students are eager to come to school and learn because her intentions are pure and honest.

When high student motivation leans more in favor of one teacher over the other at the same school, the students make certain that they spread the word to their friends. A teacher is quickly evaluated on Facebook before the bell rings to end the school day.

When administrators see this, they think that duplicating these successful lessons will help the less competent teachers be more successful. This mistake is made too frequently. Duplicating what works for one teacher does not necessarily transfer to the whole group. The "one size fits all" mentality falls short of the mark.

Too much money is spent on people who do not stick around long enough to see the strategy through. This implies that the root of the problem still exists but is hidden from plain sight.

Somewhat contrary to this, but more expansive, is NCATE's definition: the guiding principle of the teaching profession is that student learning is the goal.

> Educational leaders have the knowledge and ability to promote the success of all students by facilitating the development, articulation, implementation, and stewardship of a school or district vision of learning supported by

the school community. . . . These leaders have the knowledge and ability to promote the success of all students by promoting a positive school culture, providing an effective instructional program, applying best practice to student learning, and designing comprehensive professional growth plans for staff. . . . Educational leaders have the knowledge and ability to promote the success of all students by managing the organization, operations, and resources in a way that promotes a safe, efficient, and effective learning environment. . . . These leaders have the knowledge and ability to promote the success of all students by collaborating with families and other community members, responding to diverse community interests and needs, and mobilizing community resources. . . . Educational leaders have the knowledge and ability to promote the success of all students by acting with integrity, fairly, and in an ethical manner.[3]

The goal of teaching is student learning. Yet we struggle to meet that goal. Teachers trained under the umbrella of answering the call to teach is needed more now than ever in the history of our nation.

In 2008, 613,379 students dropped out of school in the United States.[4] In 2010, 7,200 students dropped out of school every day. This translates into 1.3 million students per year.[5] (See table 6.1)

Table 6.1. Status Dropout Rates of 16- through 24-Year-Olds in the Civilian, Noninstitutionalized Population, by Race/Ethnicity: Selected Years, 1980–2009

Year	Total	Race/Ethnicity				
		White	Black	Hispanic	Asian/Pacific Islander	American Indian/ Alaska Native
1980	14.1	11.4	19.1	35.2	—	—
1985	12.6	10.4	15.2	27.6	—	—
1990	12.1	9.0	13.2	32.4	4.9	16.4!
1995	12.0	8.6	12.1	30.0	3.9	13.4!
1998	11.8	7.7	13.8	29.5	4.1	11.8
1999	11.2	7.3	12.6	28.6	4.3	‡
2000	10.9	6.9	13.1	27.8	3.8	14.0
2001	10.7	7.3	10.9	27.0	3.6	13.1
2002	10.5	6.5	11.3	25.7	3.9	16.8
2003	9.9	6.3	10.9	23.5	3.9	15.0
2004	10.3	6.8	11.8	23.8	3.6	17.0
2005	9.4	6.0	10.4	22.4	2.9	14.0
2006	9.3	5.8	10.7	22.1	3.6	14.7
2007	8.7	5.3	8.4	21.4	6.1	19.3
2008	8.0	4.8	9.9	18.3	4.4	14.6
2009	8.1	5.2	9.3	17.6	3.4	13.2

Source: U.S. Department of Education, National Center for Education Statistics. (2011). *The Condition of Education 2011* (NCES 2011-033).

We can only achieve real change if we count on individuals at the forefront of innovation and original thinking. These individuals are the gifted people discussed earlier who have answered the call to teach. Gifted teachers would:

- Help to motivate students
- Nurture other potential teachers
- Spark a natural inquiry for learning
- Teach the holistic child
- Reach hard-to-teach children

When children begin school, at about age five, they like going to a place where they can be social. Being social is a human quality. More than that, being social is a human need. Somewhere along the way, children turn away from learning. What happens between age five and age twelve? Something is going on, to the point that it must be addressed—because this is the time that we see most of the failures in school, and see children who are choosing to drop out.

The solutions we choose must involve keeping up with the World Wide Web and global connections. If the standards do not include an intricate working of global connections, our schools will remain in "catch-up" mode.

· 7 ·

Achieving Equality

> It is easier to build strong children than to repair broken men.
>
> —Frederick Douglass

Children embrace honesty. They do not need any more studies done on their behavior. Simply, the studies cannot keep pace with the wide world of technology. If we attempt to reform education based on school data, we would be acting in a 10-year retrospective mode. The global world is moving too fast for the results of our studies. These external pressures affect the motivation of individuals in various ways:

- Health (mortality rates, diseases)
- Employment
- Cultural pressures—social mobility
  - Vocations
  - Crime
  - Living conditions
  - Ethical/moral perspectives
  - Heritage/history
- Education ethics
- Investments
- Contributions to society
- Individual worth
- Generational dialogue

Education is a means to an end. But, how many people can see the end? For some, the end may be for someone else. At least, this is what the data indicates. Education can also be viewed as a "changing" of behavior to meet a desirable direction. So, which definition works best? What does our country need from students?

1. We need students to want to learn.
2. We need students to be competent in academics (reading, writing, logical thinking).
3. We need students to become workers and to give back to society.
4. We need students to become good citizens (participate in the democratic process).
5. We need students to be moral people.
6. We need students to be innovative.
7. We need students to develop original thought.
8. We need students to carry on the process of academia.

Children do not start school as young people hating school. Generally, children like to interact with other children. As they move along toward middle school, the need for school loses its edge. Is the curriculum flow answering the needs of the students?

We must recognize the "spirit" that education brings to our children. For a great many students, having a great education does not guarantee that they can leave their neighborhoods. Limited mobility is one of the problems that education has created. The "pie in the sky" outcome is only for a few. That is the reality. The "bone of education" dangles in front—giving some a false sense of a glorious future.

When students graduate from college, the natural expectation is a fair shake at the jobs for which they apply. This fantasy lasts until the first door is slammed because the person who is hired does not have the credentials for the job—because he's somebody's relative. In the everyday world, this behavior happens all too often. Before the world of the Internet, this reality went virtually unnoticed.

Today, information travels so fast that the "real deal" is easy to see. The real deal is spoken about in music. This "real deal" is about the hypocrisy that too many of our talented youth experience on a daily basis. The children know. They also know that they are responsible for staying in school, because it's the law. In the meantime, they defy rules and make teaching almost an impossible task. This newfound revelation has turned into anger. They feel betrayed.

Until equality, which is a serious component of our education system, is reached—no child will totally reach her potential. We will forever deal with children dropping out of school and schools that churn out nonfunctional individuals into society. Until equality is fostered for all, we will continue seeing the decline of worker productivity, an increase in crime, a struggling economy, a breakdown in the family unit, a decline in the thirst for knowledge, and (most importantly) a decline in creative innovation.

We must admit that the single cure to what ails America, which is facing the challenge of educating our children, is to acknowledge that the initial structure was not designed to educate all people—and then to FIX IT. The first public schools were built to educate the wealthy and a select few. (See table 7.1)

One of the misconceptions about money is that it solves all the education problems. Money alone cannot remedy what ails America's schools. The one thing that money does is open up the gap between the haves and the have-nots.

Are the youth of today retaliating against this lie? Of course they are. Children are in a state of great need right now. Their actions say that they understand. Their music tells us so. It should not be a mystery to anyone who knows children and relates to children on a daily basis that they are crying out to be heard. Could their behavior be saying to us that they understand the truth?

When policies are adopted, do you ever wonder if anyone asked the children? In some cases, the children have revealed to us that our system is way behind the mark. For instance, students claim that the "don't" rules need to disappear. The word "no" is the magic word: no cell phones, no texting, and no music devices.

Table 7.1. Expenditures Per Pupil, Fiscal Year 2008

School District	Expenditures Per Pupil ($)
New York City	22,071
Montgomery, MD	18,011
Philadelphia	16,389
Los Angeles	14,7868
Palm Beach, FL	13,605
Baltimore	12,773
Chicago	12,126
Clark County, NV	11,859
Broward County, FL	11,569
San Diego	11,540
Jefferson County, KY	10,877
Wake County, NC	10,831
Houston	9,867
Mesa, AZ	8,257
Alpine, UT	6,858

Source: U.S. Department of Education, National Center for Education Statistics, Common Core of Data (CCD), "School District Finance Survey" (F-33), FY 2008, and "National Public Education Financial Survey," (NPEFS), 2007–08. http://nces.ed.gov/pubs2010/100largest0809/tables/table_a14.asp?referrer=report.

There is always room for a certain amount of control, but it is important to recognize the "small" stuff. On one hand, we impress upon our students the need to use technology, but tie their hands when they do. Critics of cell phones and music devices do not know how to manage a classroom. For, if they really relate to children, there would be too much engagement and no free time for goofing off.

The more money students receive for resources, the more they expect. This is one reason "rich" schools keep getting richer and the poorer schools can only hope for crumbs. How can one public school have nine tennis courts and another one have none?

Equality is not stressed enough. We've had this court battle already. After World War II, our country was still divided based on race and was faced with competing with Russia for the race to the moon.

Our education system became focused on completion. Our citizens were given the privilege of using federal funding to attend college after the Vietnam War. So, our emphasis shifted to school-to-work methods. During the 1960s and 1970s, the nation took a turn toward implementing court orders to integrate our schools.

We spent the 1980s getting the country to buy into the mindset of accepting an entire race of people as United States citizens. How can we not be behind? The simple truth is that we have lost a lot of ground by fighting ideologies, establishing personal value systems, and creating political philosophies.

This "invisible" rope is choking our youth. Making a difference in the outcome of educating future generations means that we must motivate and inspire in order to teach effectively. That means that we must pursue talented teachers. Anything less than this would be wasting our time.

A competent teacher will know what to do for the child once he enters into the room. That's the giftedness that makes the difference.

Let's take a look at the four major aspects of our current goal of fostering gifed teachers in the classroom:

1. Knowledge and skills
2. Professional disposition
3. Field experience
4. Diversity

Knowledge and skills are stressed to provide the public with the assurance that teachers know enough information to teach children. Our institutions support this by producing certificates, which indicate that the teacher took a test and passed it. Testing companies receive substantial profits from students and teacher candidates taking tests. And the public is convinced that test scores are the leading indicator of school success.

Professional disposition is a quality that does not have to be explained to talented teachers. The mere fact of having this in place is an indication that we are allowing people to enter into a profession for which they are not suited. People who answer the call to teach would find having to learn this unnecessary—because the quality is already there.

Field experience is always a positive aspect of any objective. The new proposal would expand the length of practical classroom experience into every year of preparation study. The gifted teacher has what it takes. However, each school has its own unique way of operating.

Diversity is discussed at length. As the statistics claim, there are more minority students suffering in our classrooms than white students. The obvious mode of attack used by agents of accountability make the claim that teachers should be provided with staff development to eradicate hidden biases.

Common sense would tell us that we do not have the power to change what is inside of a person's heart. But, we can discover this ahead of time instead of wasting taxpayers' money for staff development. After about five years, a freshman teacher makes the clear observation: "I do not belong in the classroom."

How do we prevent a person from spending five years of his life seeking an answer to "What am I going to be when I grow up?"

This is the REAL challenge. We must replace the traditional model with a structure that would provide us with people who are best suited for the classroom (see table 7.2).

There are numerous tests that could be used to determine whether a person is suited for the classroom. Students take profile surveys and assessments all the time. The same process can be used for teacher candidates. At

Table 7.2. New Structure of Teacher Training.

Old Model	Replace with New Structure
Knowledge and skills	Knowledge and skills + extensive self-reflection assessments (determine after one year if person has the gift to teach)
Professional disposition	Talented teachers form cooperative groups to expand and polish innovative thinking
Field experience	Field experience preserved and expanded throughout the lifetime of the preparation program
Diversity	No need for diversity training; people answering the call to teach operate with holistic thinking

present, anyone interested in pursuing education as a major in college only has to enroll and be accepted. No one bothers to screen these applicants.

Once enrolled, the candidate receives a list of requirements, including grade requirements for each course. If the person passes the courses with acceptable grades, she can enter the classroom. The next step is passing the state test.

The new proposal outlined here would make the requirements much more stringent.

1. All candidates would be required to take a "profile" test before being accepted into the education program.
2. All candidates would spend extensive time in the field, writing very detailed reflections.
3. All candidates would be under advisement of a Committee of Instruction.
4. All candidates would be required to submit an original document expressing their view of classroom teaching.
5. All candidates would be required to participate in a cooperative group (homogenous field) throughout the time spent in the preparation program.

Look at the reality. What we have now is not addressing the true need for innovation, original thinking, and preserving the value of education. But with this new structure, we can turn our education around immediately.

• 8 •

Testing Teachers

> Education is that whole system of human training within and without the schoolhouse walls, which molds and develops men.
>
> —W. E. B. Du Bois

*T*ake a close look around. Almost every aspect of education involves some sort of testing. Ever since the No Child Left Behind Act went into effect, state, local, and federal entities have been immersed in rigorous testing practices.

Some states have designed their own tests. All of this means money for somebody. Testing is big business in America. According to Adam Newman, vice president and service director for Outsell, the testing business rakes in about $2.6 billion dollars every year.[1] What person would not want a chunk of that pie? Let's not forget that money can also be made from test preparation materials, tutoring, and special classes for getting ready for the big day. Every year, parents purchase test materials. Tutors make a lot of money. Online testing materials are utilized. Special preparation companies take in hundreds of students to get them "test ready."

However, there is currently a trend to dissuade students from taking state tests. The video "Bartleby Project 2011"[2] brings to light the fact that students do have the right to refuse to take a test. Walking through the halls of most schools around testing time reveals that around testing time "incentives" are used to entice students to perform well. In a world of gifted instruction, there would be an intrinsic motivation toward wanting to succeed.

A school's Annual Year Progress (AYP) report involves taking a snapshot of students who perform well on tests. This report is made public for community review. Federal and state dollars may also be tied to a school's performance. And, again, it all boils down to money.

Money drives the entire nation. Now, education is actually a part of our Gross National Product. Standardized testing services contract for millions of dollars in every state. Think about it. There is no end to the possibilities of charging for taking a test. In a number of cases, the tests are taken over and over again by individuals who fail the first time.

High school students are "tied" to tests in order to graduate. The schools tell students that the test score is mandatory for a diploma, when in actuality the only requirement is passing classes. Remember, public schools were designed as feeders to colleges and universities in America.

A college professor can determine his stay as long as students continue getting accepted into the school. Are we doing our children a grave disservice? For one thing, not all students will succeed in college. Yet, vocational education in public schools is disappearing. When we examine the dropout rate, we must consider the dynamics of everything that is a "standard" part of a public school. Not every student will attend college.

Since its inception, testing has been controversial. Our country has come a long way from the Intelligence Quotient (IQ) testing days; however, we continue to subject children to a school career of testing. Lesson plans and testing materials are geared toward "passing the test." That's the bottom line.

Ironically, we prepare our teacher candidates for certification, but we cannot tell if they have any issues with children. If we are truly serious about education in this country, then we have to take time to utilize every method available to assure that our instructors are safe, fair-minded, non-biased people, competent in their area of expertise. However the following findings show how certification relates to teaching quality:[3]

1. A qualified teacher is not necessarily an effective teacher.
2. Policies to enhance teacher quality must be evaluated in terms of their effect on student achievement.
3. Students of first- or second-year teachers, for example, consistently do worse than those of more experienced teachers.
4. Some teachers who score higher on certification exams and some who attend more competitive undergraduate institutions produce larger performance gains for their children. The body of research that examines this issue is limited, so this finding should only be considered suggestive.
5. Teachers appear to be more effective with students of their own race or ethnicity.
6. Certified teachers are not consistently more effective than uncertified teachers, older teachers are not more effective than younger teachers, and teachers with advanced degrees are not more effective than those without such degrees.
7. Not all teachers are the same.

· 9 ·

Becoming Your Call

> The shoe that fits one person pinches another; there is no recipe for living that suits all cases.
>
> —Carl Jung

One of the most important aspects of choosing to teach is to fully understand the true nature of what being a teacher means. People do know what they are called to do—even at a young age.

The "age of reason" has been determined to be the time of a person's life when some important decisions are formed.[1] More importantly, this is also a time when unspoken questions abound. This is a critical point for the teacher and the child.

The "Eight Secrets of Success" as presented by Richard St. John may give us a little insight into what makes a great teacher:[2]

1. Passion
2. Work
3. Good
4. Focus
5. Push
6. Serve
7. Ideas
8. Persist

Deciding to become what we are called to do involves courage and conviction. But most of all, it involves understanding who we are.

The Critical Point of Recognition (CPR)[3] is the point at which a decision must be made. If not, questions will linger for a long time and the quality of our lives may be affected.

Barry Schwartz's "Paradox of Choice"[4] describes the phenomenon of having too many choices. The idea that having too many choices paralyzes us, increases our tendency toward regret, and subtracts from our happiness quotient. This bears mentioning because this paradox lies at the central position of identifying gifted teachers.

There are some people who may reach their CPR before others. This means that teachers must be able to recognize a child with a particular inclination toward the vocation of teaching.

The dropout rate may be a reflection of our children being paralyzed with too many choices. Instead of them making a choice and feeling uneasy, they quit. The psychology certainly fits.

Answering a call and becoming what you are meant to be takes courage. This choice should be made with no regrets. A person with a calling to teach has to overcome external forces before the path is cleared to actually fulfilling the mission.

The fact that our dropout rate is so high points to the fact that our classrooms are filled with teachers who missed their CPR.

On the other hand, there are children who come to their CPR and may immediately look to a called teacher—the "ah-ha moment." Deciding to pursue a vocation to teach becomes easy. The child has a model, has support, and has a mentor.

In order to meet as many children at their crossroads (at their CPR) as possible, there are two important factors to consider:

1. The CPR begins in the primary grades
2. Our classrooms should be filled with teachers serving in a vocation mode and not in a career mode

Each person has her own fingerprint. Each person has her own gifts. The gift of teaching is a unique gift because it can sometimes be mistaken as a gift for a variety of vocations. This is one reason that people miss their calling to teach.

Any person with a true command of her knowledge has the potential to impart knowledge to children. This is only a part of the equation to teaching. It's the "fingerprint" that a gifted teacher gives to her work that separates what she does from what may be happening across the hall.

Each teacher is different. That difference should be celebrated and encouraged. Training people to become teachers only satisfies a tiny fraction of what it takes to make a great teacher.

Being a teacher means that a person is good at almost everything she attempts. But, the point that separates this gift from others is the life commitment. A life commitment entails true inner reflection. The life commitment makes it real.

A true teacher "wears" her role 24/7. Children look for consistency. A constant nature helps children learn. They respect teachers who pay attention to a routine, which is both creative and constructive.

Teaching as a vocation is about serving others. For gifted teachers, the eight secrets to success flow in this order:

1. Serve
2. Good
3. Passion
4. Focus
5. Push
6. Work
7. Ideas
8. Persist

The notion of choosing the right vocation is not a new one. A 1917 book by Holmes Merton makes the claim: "Oftentimes the best training for a misfit calling does not enable a man even to earn his salt in that calling, whereas the same man might rise to eminence in the vocation which called his dominant abilities into play."[5]

• 10 •

Recruiting and Retaining the Best Teachers

> The teacher who is indeed wise does not bid you to enter the house of his wisdom but rather leads you to the threshold of your mind.
>
> —Khalil Gibran

The scientific formula for recruiting and retaining the best teachers must consider the following attributes of the system:

- Children are fluid entities.
- The "system" is continually moving.
- Certain variables (politics, policy, laws) restrict growth.
- The system is not conducive to open points of entry.

When conducting scientific experiments, it becomes necessary to set a formal hypothesis based on observations of a pattern that we do not understand. An inherent flaw in critical analyses of what makes schools work or what makes a great teacher is to assume that there are no great teachers.

Nothing could be further from the truth. There are children born everyday who are gifted to teach. The training institutions deal with adults who "think" that they want to teach.

The data we collect today is already old. If we study children from the seventh grade through graduation, that group is gone. We can only get a glimpse at what patterns develop if we repeated the same steps over and over again.

Once an inherent flaw enters into the experimental stage, or when collecting or analyzing data, we are doomed before we get out of the gate. At this point, it is imperative that we set up a new method of determining what works. Some people have been skeptical of the notion that great teachers possess this "magic" that is solely for them and for no one else.

Honestly, we have to look at the results. Results matter. Despite the struggle of some agencies to dismiss this "magic," the children know the difference.

Children respond to sincerity.

Over 500 students (mostly at the middle and high school level) were asked to describe what a great teacher looks like.[1] This study was conducted with public and Catholic school students over a period of 22 years. Here are their responses. Seven attributes were determined:

1. Great teachers laugh at themselves. They have a sense of humor that far exceeds that of the average classroom teacher.
2. Great teachers are nurturing. They show compassion and sympathy for others. They are fair to everyone.
3. Great teachers have "unique" hands. Children look at the physical hands of teachers to determine if their touch is sincere. They describe hand motions. They can tell deliberate hand gestures from ones of "love."
4. Great teachers create an environment of happiness in the classroom. Students feel safe around them and trust them. They receive information openly from these teachers and are not afraid to engage in conversation.
5. Great teachers have a certain kind of "presence" in the room. They show confidence and project this confidence to their students.
6. Great teachers are strategic problem solvers. Students take notice of the many tasks that teachers have to deal with on a daily basis. They take notice of how teachers deal with individual students, especially the challenging students. Often, students base their relationships with teachers on how teachers deal with other people.
7. Great teachers are extremely patient people. Children understand the demands of teaching. They take notice of what buttons to push. They also know that some students thrive by unnerving teachers just to get a reaction. Patient teachers stay "outside" of the situation and not enter into it personally, but deal with matters objectively.

Over more than two decades, students consistently responded with the same answers. Students appreciated teachers who they can be with in a crisis situation. During lockdown drills, students expressed their preference for the teachers they feel close to over those from whom they feel distant.

Students can also determine how much a teacher knows about her subject area after just a few minutes of classroom instruction. They expressed the fact that the least effective teachers rely heavily on sticking to lesson plans, the textbook, or the regular order of the day.

Students stated that the most effective teachers are never caught looking in a textbook, reading a lesson plan, or avoiding "teachable moments" for the sake of sticking to a routine.

Students are saying that things like technology in the classroom matters, but that they would much more prefer having a knowledgeable teacher in the room to guide them through the process. Students respond well to teachers who trust them to think.

In the study, students expressed frustration with teachers who put themselves in the middle of "their" thinking process. As a result, they allow the teacher to give the answers and they (the students) wait. In many cases, parents selected teachers who students recommended to each other. Parents were made aware of the great teachers in the building and requested these teachers personally.

The overall climate of the room was also important to these students. They expressed the concern that not enough teachers asked them how they were feeling, what they ate for lunch, what they did over the weekend, or shared with them an interesting story.

A surprise factor from the study was how much emphasis children put on laughter inside of the classroom. Students expressed their feeling that the general nature of school is boring. They stated that they would much rather be at home taking home-schooled classes or online classes. These students preferred (and were hardly absent from) those classes where a lot of laughter was present.

Along with laughter, students respected the teachers who admitted they made mistakes or showed human emotion in the classroom. They gravitated toward these teachers because it gave them a sense of security.

Every student described a great teacher as a nurturing person, not necessarily one with children, but one who possesses a "motherly" instinct. The students described this quality as one they respected and trusted. They understood that rules would be followed and that no one was above the rest—everyone was equally loved.

Objectivity went hand-in-hand with nurturing. The students said that they crave fairness in the classroom. They described classrooms where some teachers would only teach to the "smart" students and turn their backs (physically) to those who took a little more time achieving the same goals. They described "class" punishments as grossly unfair. They made the claim that this practice creates a divide between teacher and student.

One interesting fact: the students stated that they were much smarter than the teachers knew—that they held back on purpose.

In the previous chapter, the Critical Point of Recognition (CPR) was discussed. It is important to note here that the focal point remains simplistic. Our training institutions have to accept the fact that there are people who are born to teach.

These institutions must begin going into the middle and high schools around the country to recruit future teachers. The process they are presently using relies on the person coming to them first. To some degree, this decision-making process may occur as early as elementary school.

These institutions must plant the seed early and continue revisiting classrooms until young people find it satisfying to be a teacher again.

• 11 •

Making the Choice—and Sticking to It

> Cheshire Puss, asked Alice. Would you tell me, please, which way I ought to go from here? That depends a good deal on where you want to go, said the Cat. I don't much care where, said Alice. Then it doesn't matter which way you go, said the Cat.
>
> —Charles "Lewis Carroll" Dodgson

According to Barry Schwartz,[1] children do not know enough to decide. That means that we should help them.

Students in classrooms all over this country are under tremendous pressure to perform. They realize the high stakes involved from day one. They are also told, "You can be anything you want to be." Well, what that translates into, especially in this global economy, could be one of tens of millions of things.

So, how do the students decide? There are so many careers, so many colleges, so many different jobs. Where does one begin the search? This stage can become extremely frustrating for even the brightest students.

According to Schwartz's "paradox of choice," the more options we have, the more we experience regret. It's such an excellent example of irony. Do decisions paralyze us?

Based on the study of 500 students described in the previous chapter, it is safe to say that it was observed how much students struggle with making the right decision and pleasing the adults involved in their lives.

The theory explains that if we maximize individual freedom, we maximize choice, and individual welfare is increased. This is an even more concrete sense of support for children to come into contact with teachers who have a mature mental capacity, a sincere love for learning, and a desire to teach.

If failure is not an option, then we should take whatever steps we need to ensure that our children, especially ones of preschool and elementary age, to receive not a quality education, but a holistic education.

The data we see could be a reflection of who the teachers really are. If we see that children are disruptive, then the teacher in the room is the wrong teacher for those children. What hurts that teacher more than anything is attending staff development to learn about the group of children she has, sending her back to the classroom, and expecting her to change. This may be responsible for the high attrition rate that we see in the new teacher pool.

There is nothing that can be done with a person who does not belong in the classroom. The best thing would be to allow that person to discover another line of work. However, if the training components help people discover the road they should take long before entering the classroom, this entire episode could be avoided.

Our educational system instructs us to set high expectations for the students. Yet, Schwartz tells us that one of the secrets of happiness is setting low expectations. How can this make a better and more successful student?

Stakeholders would probably not buy into hearing "low" expectations. Hearing that word automatically sends a limiting message. And, in this country, we preach to our children that getting a good education makes us free. So, how can we perform a marriage between our perceptions and reality?

When a person internalizes failure, it could lead to depression, suicide, or a lifetime of regret. None of these things is good.

Schwartz tells us that regret subtracts from happiness. He goes on to say that people, in general, have a difficult time making decisions. Why do students prefer to be told exactly what to do instead of creating their own environments for discovery?

Some teachers would state that the worksheet-driven method is the only way they can teach. If this is the case, then that teacher is not fit for the classroom. Great teachers have no difficulty in creating a setting where children can be expressive.

In science, our children must understand that we find answers by being wrong more than by being right. The "color within the lines" philosophy spills over into every area of children's lives. Children will tell you that they are very concerned about being wrong. According to Jim Taylor, "One of the most powerful ways you can encourage your children to become successful, happy, and contributing people is to teach them good decision making and then to allow them to make their own decisions."[2]

Volumes of information have been written by psychologists, leading us to believe that children do pay attention to how decisions are made for them and that they should make good decisions. We certainly do not want children feeling less satisfied from making a decision, one that may prove to be the right choice.

Schwartz explains why choice makes people miserable:

1. Regret or anticipated regret
2. Opportunity costs
3. Escalation of expectations
4. Self-blame[3]

Conclusion

> I'm not afraid of storms, for I'm learning to sail my ship.
>
> —Aeschylus

There is much to digest in these chapters. The proponents of this novel method introduce us to a whole new way to approach attracting, recruiting, and retaining great teachers in our classrooms. Outside of parenting a child, teachers have the most profound impact on children. It is our teachers who shape children's ideas and self-esteem. No one would argue that teachers do not have a tremendous impact on good and bad outcomes.

Change takes time. For our children, that time was yesterday.

The educational system under which we operate is basically a good system with fine intentions. There have been public education success stories. However, like anything that's been around for a long time, it is time for an overhaul.

Societal components, such as poverty and academic disparity, were highlighted to drive home the point that having great teachers in the classroom does matter. We can clearly see what happens as a result of not having proper instruction. Having proper teachers in our classrooms covers all the bases.

It is time that we concentrate on attracting young people to the field of teaching, exposing them to the world of teaching, holding conversations with them about teaching as a vocation, and providing support for their decision.

Family and friends act as the support mantle. A young person needs to know that she has the support of the people who matter most to her.

In reviewing the statistics for the jobs that people find the most rewarding, it is interesting to note that the type of teacher mentioned belongs to the special education group (see appendix). If you ever have a chance to speak to a special education teacher, you will discover how unique they are. Special education teachers understand that the tasks they have are no walk in the park. Yet, they choose this vocation openly and honestly. This is something for which they are aptly suited.

A lot of people are joining in the conversation about what is best to do with our education system. The proposal outlined in this book is no exception. What should be de-emphasized is the need for more experimentation. Simply put, we do not have time for that. There is enough data to indicate what the next step should be. It's up to us to stop making a somewhat easy problem into one that is difficult to solve. In the meantime, there are students trying to graduate. So, we are operating within a system that is moving along with its subjects. And we wonder why the methods are not working?

The concept of answering the call to teach should give us at least three-quarters of what we need to solve the education problem in this country. Without individuals answering the call to teach, we will be stuck with people who do not have a true idea of what children need.

Remember what the children are saying about the attributes of a great teacher? We should listen to them.

We know that children need teachers. Children need responsible teachers. Children grow with teachers who have a deep understanding of what they teach. All data points in the direction of having great teachers in the classroom to make the most impact in turning around test scores and helping children succeed.

In this book, another important piece of this picture was established. Great teachers help children during their decision-making period. Children understand far more than for which we give them credit.

A person who answers the call to teach is also adding back the value of teaching. This value has been an absent component for a long time. Few of our children with the gift to teach are opting to teach. The reasons for this were outlined earlier in the book.

We cannot turn our backs on the fact that teachers have to make a decent living. There is no logical reason that the people who help shape our citizens, encourage original thinking, and promote moral quality should be left near the end of the line. Salary alone may be the number one reason new teachers leave the classroom. This turnover is a $7 billion expense across the United States.[1]

If our mindset changes, then we will begin to see:

- More competence
- Greater retention
- More called teachers
- More consistency

- Equality in teaching
- More trust from the community
- More original ideas
- Greater student success
- Fairness
- A secured vetting process
- Fewer gaps in achievement
- Significant decreases in dropouts
- Less money spent on staff development
- Less need for funds to attract teachers

The Critical Point of Recognition (CPR) should be a point of enlightenment for each child, not a point of frustration. A teacher who is called to teach makes this transition smooth and effortless.

What we are facing is a direct result of the external influences children receive from outside of school. A child can decide her future in the very early stages of life without letting anyone know. Primary grade teachers play a huge part in the process of making value decisions.

From observations made in this book, it can be concluded that primary grade teachers set the foundation for future decisions, and that these primary grade teachers can kill dreams if children come into contact with a person who is not fit for the job.

We have tried a number of novel approaches to fixing what ails our educational system. But, we have not tried the method that religious orders use to help someone determine if that type of lifestyle is right for them.

Teaching is a lifestyle. A large number of teachers talk about bringing their work home. These "at home" activities take a long time and a large amount of time away from normal activities. It takes a special person to sacrifice that kind of time.

Our teachers deserve to know if the job fits them or not before entering the classroom. Our training institutions can easily put the missing gears in place: psychological testing, more clinical experience, and a more thorough reflective process.

It is only through the reflective process that a person will gain insight into understanding their true calling. If we continue spending hundreds of thousands of dollars on staff development to "hope" to get a teacher out of the deal, we will be doing a grave disservice to our children.

What makes sense is to fit the round peg into the round hole, instead of the square one.

Answered the Call—
Made a Difference

*H*ere are some examples of people who answered the call to teach and made a difference.

MILRED B. MARTINEZ

In 1934, a small kindergarten school was started in New Orleans, Louisiana, by a pioneer named Mildred B. Martinez. Martinez married a local bricklayer, Maurice Martinez, Sr., and had three children—Maurice, Jr., Josepha, and Numa.

Back in those days, "Negro" children were not attending schools before age five. Martinez, after working at an elite uptown New Orleans school (Newman), decided to teach her own children how to read. She could not understand why children had to wait until attending school to learn how to read.

Someone encouraged Martinez to open her own kindergarten. She did. She only had fifteen children in her first graduating class.

The "magic" of the Martinez kindergarten quickly spread throughout the city when her graduates scored high on the entrance reading test. Negroes were not expected to know that much about reading.

Martinez knew she had something. Her house, turned into a schoolhouse, grew until bursting at the seams and maintained a waiting list every year. Martinez emphasized academics, but each child who attended the Martinez School was "beautiful."

At the end of the day, a child who felt beautiful could and would do anything to succeed. The school stressed phonics. When children graduated as four-year-olds, they could read as well as seven-year-olds or older children.

The math concepts were tackled in a way so that children did not fear working with numbers. Graduates of the Martinez kindergarten could add and subtract numbers in three columns.

Music, dance, and foreign language (primarily French) were staples of the Martinez lessons. Everyone was involved—including parents. The school was run like one big family. There was a financial support system in place for families who could not afford the school.

Financial resources were put in place to assist parents in understanding how to manage their money—and how to save. Martinez insisted on excellence. Parents signed an agreement to sit with their child every night.

If parents fell short, Martinez would call "Mother." She wanted to know what she could do to prevent distractions and help the child achieve her best.

As far as honesty was concerned, Martinez was one of most frank people that ever walked the earth. She knew the goals. She paced her children and she pushed them toward those goals—the gentle push of a nurturing mother.

The Martinez School was not all academics. Children were kings and queens. At graduation time, Martinez was the first person to develop a way of fundraising that kept her school alive. Parents would hold "suppers" to raise money for their children to compete for a spot as the king or queen or a part of the royal court.

As it is with the New Orleans tradition of Mardi Gras, the friendly competition took a life of its own. Soon, Martinez gained so much recognition for her graduation ceremonies that the ceremonies were held at one of the city's auditoriums and was televised on the news.

Anybody who was anybody wanted to be a part of the Martinez School. As time progressed, private high schools began requesting Martinez kindergarten graduates.

The Amistad Research Center at Tulane University, the archival depot for historical documents for African Americans, houses the history of the Martinez School.

Before her death, national as well as international educators who observed her children and her teachers visited Martinez to discover that special element of the school and her method of teaching. She was asked, "How do you get children to respond so well?" Her response: "With love."

Today, Martinez graduates can be found all over the world in key positions.

MOTHER TERESA

On September 10, 1946, Teresa experienced what she later described as "the call within the call" while traveling by train to the Loreto convent in Darjeeling from Calcutta for her annual retreat. "I was to leave the convent and help the poor while living among them. It was an order. To fail would have been to break the faith."[1]

MARVA COLLINS

"I have discovered few learning disabled students in my three decades of teaching. I have, however, discovered many, many victims of teaching inabilities."[2]

Marva Collins is to be commended for her work with children who were labeled as learning disabled and disruptive to the learning environment. She took these underserved children and made them special. Her methods were given the highest praise. She too believed that reading was key to a child's education.

Like Martinez, Collins focused on the beauty of each child. She made children feel special, and they responded.

Appendix

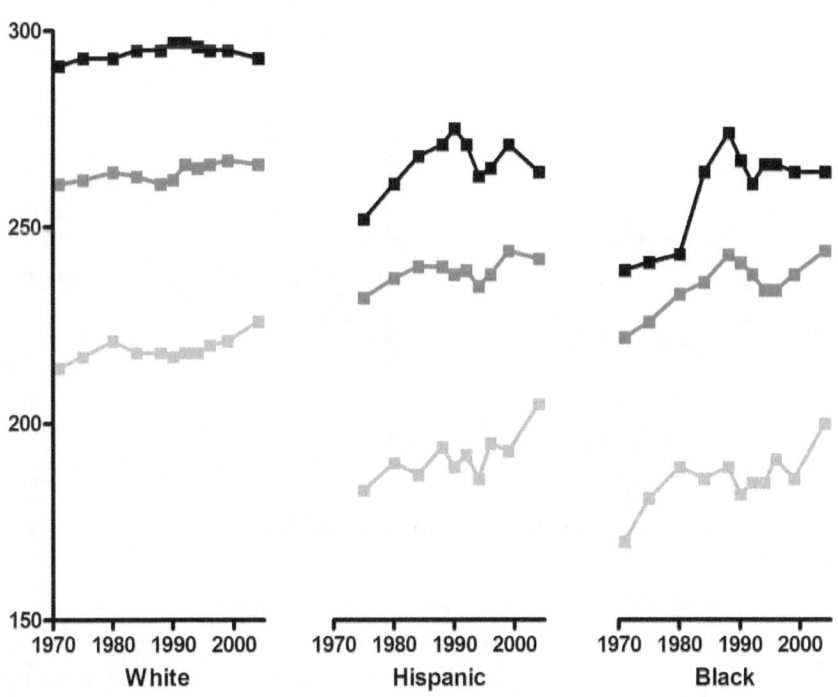

A. NATIONAL ASSESSMENT OF
EDUCATIONAL PROGRESS—READING TRENDS BY RACE

B. NATIONAL ASSESSMENT OF EDUCATIONAL PROGRESS—MATH

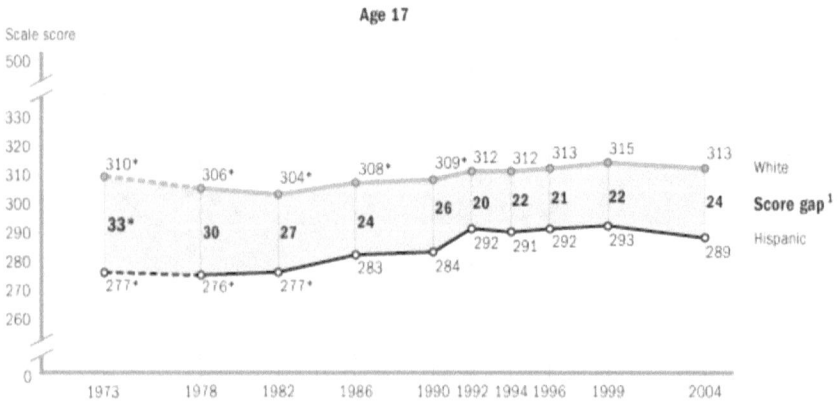

C. POVERTY STATISTICS

- In 2009, 43.6 million Americans (14.3%) lived in poverty.
- In 2009, 8.8 (11.1%) million U.S. families lived in poverty.
- In 2009, 24.7 million (12.9%) Americans aged 18–64 lived in poverty.
- In 2009, 15.5 million (20.7%) U.S. children under the age of 18 lived in poverty.
- In 2009, 3.4 million (8.9%) U.S. seniors 65 and older lived in poverty.

(Source: "Hunger and Poverty Statistics," Feeding America. http://feedingamerica.org/hunger-in-america/hunger-facts/hunger-and-poverty-statistics.aspx)

D. TOP 10 MOST GRATIFYING JOBS AND THE PERCENTAGE OF SUBJECTS WHO SAID THEY WERE VERY SATISFIED WITH THE JOB

- Clergy—87%
- Firefighters—80%
- Physical therapists—78%
- Authors—74%
- Special education teachers—70%
- Teachers—69%
- Education administrators—68%
- Painters and sculptors—67%
- Psychologists—67%
- Security and financial services salespersons—65%
- Operating engineers—64%
- Office supervisors—61%

(Source: Jeanna Bryner, "Survey Reveals Most Satisfying Jobs." LiveScience.com, April 17, 2007. http://www.livescience.com/1431-survey-reveals-satisfying-jobs.html)

E. 10 LEAST GRATIFYING JOBS, WHERE FEW PARTICIPANTS REPORTED BEING VERY SATISFIED

- Laborers, except construction—21%
- Apparel clothing salespersons—24%
- Hand packers and packagers—24%
- Food preparers—24%
- Roofers—25%
- Cashiers—25%
- Furniture and home-furnishing salespersons—25%
- Bartenders—26%
- Freight, stock and material handlers—26%
- Waiters and servers—27%

(Source: Bryner, "Survey Reveals Most Satisfying Jobs.")

F. JOBS HELD BY PEOPLE SCORING HIGHEST ON THE HAPPINESS SCALE

- Clergy
- Firefighters

- Transportation ticket and reservation agents
- Housekeepers and butlers
- Hardware/building supplies salespersons
- Architects
- Mechanics and repairers
- Special education teachers
- Actors and directors
- Science technicians

(Source: Bryner, "Survey Reveals Most Satisfying Jobs.")

G. LABOR FORCE STATUS OF 2008–2009 HIGH SCHOOL DROPOUTS AND COMPLETERS NOT ENROLLED IN COLLEGE: 2009

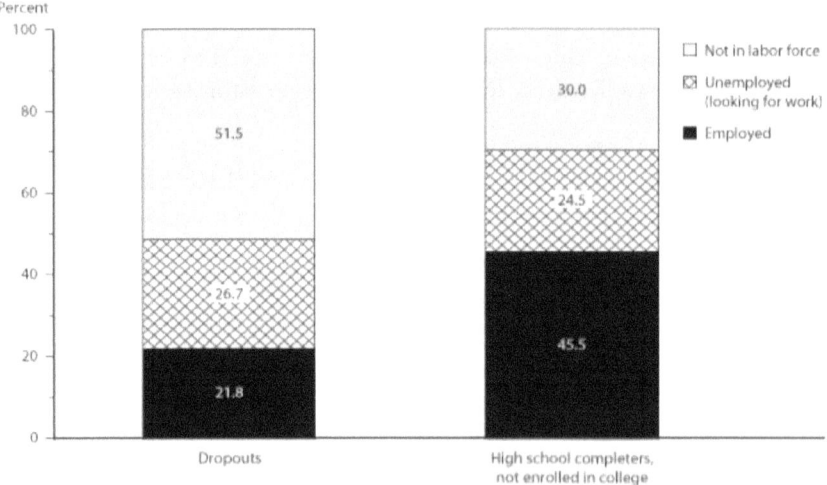

(Source: National Center for Education Statistics, "Digest of Education Statistics 2010, Figure 23." NCES 2011-015, April 2011. http://nces.ed.gov/programs/digest/d10/figures/fig_23.asp?referrer=figures.)

H. PUBLIC DIRECT EXPENDITURES ON EDUCATION AS A PERCENTAGE OF GROSS DOMESTIC PRODUCT (GDP), BY COUNTRY: 2007

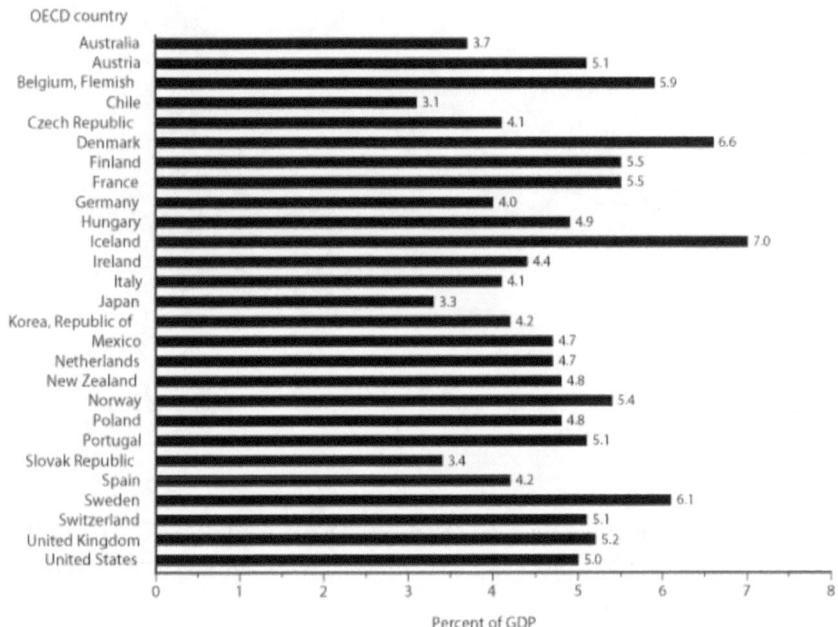

(Source: National Center for Education Statistics, "Digest of Education Statistics 2010, Figure 28." NCES 2011-015, April 2011. http://nces.ed.gov/programs/digest/d10/figures/fig_28.asp?referrer=figures.)

I. TOTAL AND FULL-DAY PREPRIMARY ENROLLMENT OF THREE- TO FIVE-YEAR-OLDS: 1970–2009

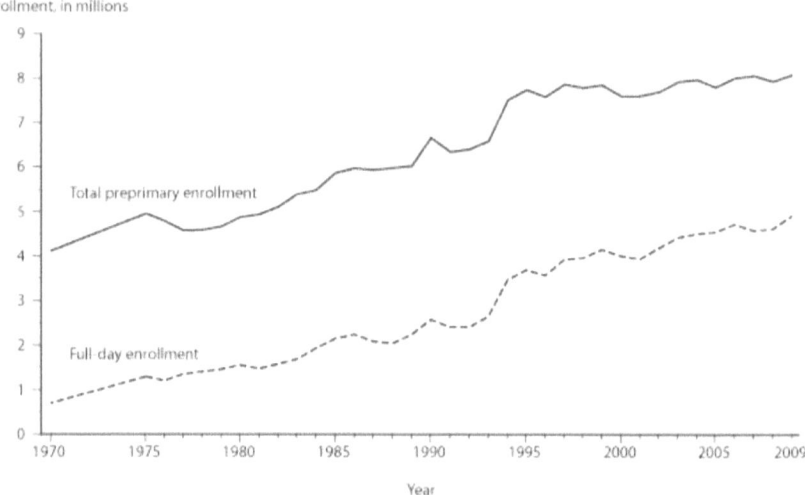

(Source: National Center for Education Statistics, "Digest of Education Statistics 2010, Figure 7." 2010 NCES Tables and Figures, http://nces.ed.gov/programs/digest/d10/figures/fig_07.asp.)

Notes

INTRODUCTION

1. Elizabeth Green, "Building a Better Teacher." *New York Times*, March 7, 2010. http://www.nytimes.com/2010/03/07/magazine/07Teachers-t.html?pagewanted=all.
2. Eric Hanushek, Stanford University, from "Creating a New Teaching Profession," Dr. Doug Green at www.drdouggreen.com/wp-content/Creating-New-Profession.pdf.

CHAPTER 1

1. "FAQs—And Honest Answers." Sisters of St. Joseph of Concordia, Kansas. http://www.csjkansas.org/want-to-know-more-about-religious-life/faqs/.
2. Phil Izzo, "Number of the Week: U.S. Teachers' Hours among World's Longest." *Wall Street Journal*, June 25, 2011. http://blogs.wsj.com/economics/2011/06/25/number-of-the-week-u-s-teachers-hours-among-worlds-longest/.
3. Elizabeth Green, "Building a Better Teacher." *New York Times*, March 7, 2010. http://www.nytimes.com/2010/03/07/magazine/07Teachers-t.html?pagewanted=all.
4. "Salary for All K–12 Teachers." Payscale.com, January 26, 2012. http://www.payscale.com/research/US/All_K-12_Teachers/Salary.
5. "Salary for People with Doctor of Medicine (MD) degrees." Payscale.com, January 26, 2012. http://www.payscale.com/research/US/People_with_Doctor_of_Medicine_%28MD%29_Degrees/Salary.
6. Jeffrey Taylor, Marcia B. Harris, and Susan Taylor, "Parents Have Their Say . . . about Their College-age Children's Career Decisions." *NACE Journal of Career Planning and Employment*, Winter 2004.

CHAPTER 2

1. "Egyptian Maths." YouTube video, posted September 5, 2008. www.youtube.com/watch?v=Ih1ZWE3pe9o.
2. Christine Collier, Judith Johnson, Lisa Nyberg, Virginia Lockwood, "Learning Science Through Inquiry," www.learner.org/workshops/inquiry/resources/faq.html.
3. "Egyptian Maths."
4. Sandra Wozniak, "Does Spelling Count?" Edutopia.org, April 6, 2011. www.edutopia.org/groups/middle-school/49793.
5. "Major: Education," The College Board, 2012, www.collegeboard.com/csearch/majors_careers/profiles/majors/13.0101.html.

CHAPTER 3

1. All of these quotes can be found at http://answers.yahoo.com/question/index?qid=20070526125741AAkKRk8.

CHAPTER 4

1. Amanda Ripley, "What makes a great teacher?" *Atlantic,* January/February 2010, http://www.theatlantic.com/magazine/archive/2010/01/what-makes-a-great-teacher/7841/.
2. Heather Hill and David Cohen, "Teaching Teachers: Professional Development to Improve Student Achievement," *Research Points*, Summer 2005, Volume 3 Issue 1.
3. Thomas Corcoran, "Helping Teachers Teach Well." *CPRE Policy Briefs*, June 1995. Consortium for Policy Research in Education, www.cpre.org/images/stories/cpre_pdfs/rb16.pdf.

CHAPTER 5

1. "Many High School Students Bored in Class: Survey." Reuters, February 28, 2007. http://www.reuters.com/article/2007/02/28/us-usa-students-survey-idUSN2724246420070228.
2. Jeanna Bryner, "Most students bored at school." Live Science, February 28, 2007. http://www.livescience.com/1308-students-bored-school.html.

3. "100+ Motivational Techniques to Take Learning to the Next Level." Smart-Teaching.org, August 6, 2008. http://www.smartteaching.org/blog/2008/08/100-motivational-techniques-to-take-learning-to-the-next-level/.
4. http://edtech.kennesaw.edu/intech/cooperativelearning.htm.

CHAPTER 6

1. Project Implicit home page, projectimplicit.net/index.php.
2. National Council for Accreditation of Teacher Education (NCATE), *Professional Standards for the Accreditation of Teacher Preparation Institutions*. NCATE, 2008.
3. NCATE, *Professional Standards*.
4. "Public School Graduates and Dropouts from the Common Core of Data: School Year 2007–2008." U.S. Department of Education, National Center of Education Statistics, June 2010. http://nces.ed.gov/pubs2010/2010341.pdf.
5. Patrice Wingert, "The (Somewhat) Good and (Mostly) Bad News about High School Dropout Rates. *Newsweek*, June 13, 2010. http://www.newsweek.com/blogs/the-gaggle/2010/06/14/the-somewhat-good-and-mostly-bad-news-about-high-school-dropout-rates.html.

CHAPTER 8

1. Adam Newman, NBR transcripts, February 11, 2008, on www.pbs.org/nbr/site/onair/transcripts/080218a/.
2. "Bartleby Project 2011: Do Not Take Your State Tests!" YouTube video, posted September 19, 2010. www.youtube.com/watch?v=AWqdScvrKCo.
3. Brian Jacob, "The Challenges of Staffing Urban Schools with Effective Teachers." *Work and Family*, 17 (1), Spring 2007. www.futureofchildren.org/publications/journals/article/index.xml?journalid=34&articleid=79&sectionid=464.

CHAPTER 9

1. J. Delany, "Age of Reason." The Catholic Encyclopedia, 1907. New Advent .org. http://www.newadvent.org/cathen/01209a.htm.
2. Richard St. John, "Richard St. John's 8 Secrets of Success." TED: Ideas Worth Spreading video, posted December 2006. http://www.ted.com/talks/lang/en/richard_st_john_s_8_secrets_of_success.html.

3. This is data that the author collected.

4. Barry Schwartz, "Barry Schwartz on the Paradox of Choice." TED: Ideas Worth Spreading video, posted September 2006. http://www.ted.com/talks/barry_schwartz_on_the_paradox_of_choice.html.

5. Holmes Merton, *How to Choose the Right Vocation: Vocational Self-Measurement Based Upon Natural Abilities.* Charleston, SC: Nabu Press, 2010 (originally published 1917).

CHAPTER 10

1. This is the author's own study.

CHAPTER 11

1. Barry Schwartz, "Barry Schwartz on the Paradox of Choice." Video posted on TED: Ideas Worth Spreading, September 2006. http://www.ted.com/talks/barry_schwartz_on_the_paradox_of_choice.html.

2. Jim Taylor, "Lesson #1: Make Good Decisions." *Family Online Magazine.* http://www.familiesonlinemagazine.com/kids-decision-making.html.

3. Schwartz, "Paradox of Choice."

CONCLUSION

1. Lisa Lambert, "Half of Teachers Quit in Five Years." Washingtonpost.com, May 9, 2006. http://www.washingtonpost.com/wp-dyn/content/article/2006/05/08/AR2006050801344.html.

ANSWERED THE CALL

1. "Mother Theresa." Wikipedia. http://en.wikipedia.org/wiki/Mother_Teresa.

2. "Marva Collins." Wikipedia. http://en.wikipedia.org/wiki/Marva_Collins.

About the Author

Charlese E. Brown, a New Orleans native and graduate of Xavier University of Louisiana, has been a classroom instructor for over 20 years.